The Library and Its Users

Recent Titles in
Contributions in Librarianship and Information Science

Librarianship: A Third World Perspective
Rosario Gassol de Horowitz

Pascal Programming for Libraries: Illustrative Examples for Information Specialists
Charles H. Davis, Gerald W. Lundeen, and Debora Shaw

The Culture and Control of Expertise: Toward a Sociological Understanding of Librarianship
Michael F. Winter

The American Public Library and the Problem of Purpose
Patrick Williams

Public Librarianship: An Issues-Oriented Approach
Verna L. Pungitore

Naturalistic Inquiry for Library Science: Methods and Applications for Research, Evaluation, and Teaching
Constance Ann Mellon

From Documentation to Information Science: The Beginning and Early Development of the American Documentation Institute—American Society for Information Science
Irene S. Farkas-Conn

The Decision-Making Process for Library Collections: Case Studies in Four Types of Libraries
Beatrice Kovacs

The Librarian, the Scholar, and the Future of the Research Library
Eldred Smith

Social Science Reference Sources: A Practical Guide
Revised and Enlarged Second Edition
Tze-chung Li

Books and Blueprints: Building America's Public Libraries
Donald E. Oehlerts

Dilemmas in the Study of Information: Exploring the Boundaries of Information Science
S. D. Neill

THE LIBRARY AND ITS USERS

The Communication Process

JOHN M. BUDD

Contributions in Librarianship and Information Science, Number 71
Paul Wasserman, Series Adviser

GREENWOOD PRESS
New York • Westport, Connecticut • London

Copyright Acknowledgment

Material reprinted by permission of Greenwood Publishing Group, Inc., Westport, CT, from *Overload & Boredom: Essays in the Information Society*, by Orrin E. Klapp. Copyright © 1986 by Orrin E. Klapp. Published in 1986 by Greenwood Press.

Library of Congress Cataloging-in-Publication Data

Budd, John M.
The library and its users : the communication process / John M. Budd.
p. cm.—(Contributions in librarianship and information science, ISSN 0084-9243 ; no. 71)
Includes bibliographical references and index.
ISBN 0-313-28153-X (alk. paper)
1. Libraries and readers. 2. Communication in library science. 3. Libraries—Communication systems. I. Title. II. Series.
Z711.B925 1992
025.5—dc20 91-42732

British Library Cataloguing in Publication Data is available.

Library of Congress Catalog Card Number: 91-42732
ISBN: 0-313-28153-X
ISSN: 0084-9243

First published in 1992

Greenwood Press, 88 Post Road West, Westport, CT 06881
An imprint of Greenwood Publishing Group, Inc.

Printed in the United States of America

The paper used in this book complies with the Permanent Paper Standard issued by the National Information Standards Organization (Z39.48-1984).

10 9 8 7 6 5 4 3 2 1

This book is dedicated to Les Asheim, who influenced it in its entirety, whether he knows it or not.

Contents

Tables and Figures

TABLES

FIGURES

Preface

This may seem like an idiosyncratic book. Most library literature is "home-grown"; that is, it uses the work done only by contributors to the library and information science field. While I am not faulting that tendency, many other contributions have relevance to the endeavors of librarians. The primary drawback to incorporating this larger literature into our work is the enormity of that literature. A cursory examination reveals that it is, indeed, a daunting task to sift through the work of other fields and to adopt some portion of it into our own. This is an extended caveat. I have attempted to borrow from several literatures—those of communication, information theory, philosophy, linguistics, and others—to further a discussion of the communication process of which libraries and librarians are part. I do not pretend that any section of this book represents a full coverage of these other literatures, or that the works cited here are the only works of relevance to us and what we do. No one book could possibly incorporate everything of relevance.

This book may also seem idiosyncratic because of its focus. It should be self-evident that libraries and librarians are part of a very large communication system. In fact, the library itself is a communication system. Why does anyone need to be told this? While libraries and librarians exist to communicate and to foster communication, we sometimes forget that part of our existence. We need, too, to be cognizant of the complexities of communication and to realize that the communication engaged in by a library has many facets and nuances. So, the primary purpose of this book is to examine the library and the librarian as they communicate with their reason for existence, the user.

The first two chapters set the tone for what is to follow. They provide some background, first about libraries and their history and purpose, then about information theory and human communication theory. These latter two are important to an understanding of the stuff of libraries, the materials collected and their contents, and to the possible ways this stuff may be used. This stuff—let us call it information for lack of a better word—is indeed multifarious. Almost all libraries collect information of various types—numerous subjects, forms of content, genres—and in various media. This alone creates complexity, especially for the user, who is likely to have an imperfect vision of what the library *can* provide. The background material also addresses some important problems and potential problems. Where things are designed to function, there is still the possibility of dysfunction. Part of the cause of library dysfunction is societal; there is more information than can be assimilated by anyone. The growth of volume and variety of formats is a definite hurdle for both library and user.

If the library is to function as a communication mechanism, then we should be aware of some of the possible shapes and forms communication can take. To come to a better understanding of this, several models of the communication process are presented. Some of these will have greater utility to us than others, but we must examine them critically in order to arrive at some sort of judgment. Once this is accomplished, we must look at the place of the library and of the librarian in these schemes. We must ask how each entity functions as a source of information (or at least as the sender of a message), as the receiver of a message, and as a channel. The roles of the library and the librarian are, of necessity, fluid so that success of the process is more probable. These roles will be addressed in separate chapters.

Then, the bane of communication—noise—will be explored. Does the library help to eliminate noise for the user? Or does it create noise and hinder use? The same questions can be asked of the librarian. What are the manifestations of noise? In tackling these questions, I present some alternatives and contingencies for librarians to consider. I hope that the readers of this book will be introduced to some different approaches to the functioning of libraries and will come to an appreciation of the value of the larger literature related to our business.

Acknowledgments

I bent a lot of ears while working on this book. To these people, who I hope are still friends, I say thank you. Their help and encouragement have been invaluable as this project progressed, and their suggestions were always appreciated. Special thanks go to Anne Moss and Charley Seavey, who read drafts of this, either in whole or in part. I am also grateful to Vivian Auld, whose help with graphics has been invaluable. Their criticisms made this a better work.

Very special thanks to Les Asheim. In classes and in conversation he planted the germs of what has taken substantive form here. Sometimes his influence was direct, especially with regard to communication theory. At other times his influence was less direct. If I have been able to become something of a critical thinker, I owe much of that development to him. His influence extends well beyond the bounds of this book, as his students and friends well know.

The Library and Its Users

1

Introduction

HOW WE CAME TO BE HERE

In their text on building library collections, Arthur Curley and Dorothy Broderick state, "Libraries exist to facilitate communication whether that be between persons in the present or from someone in the past to someone in the present or from someone in the present to some future person."[1] Explicit in their statement is the importance of the process of communication, which will be the primary focus of this discourse. There is another, implicit, concept in the Curley and Broderick definition of the purpose of libraries—information. If we accept that the facilitation of communication of information suffices as a capsule view of libraries, then the basic question that follows is: How does this occur? This book is an effort to address that question. Of course, an understanding of the environment—libraries—should precede any discussion.

For most of their collective life libraries have housed artifacts. This was true for the Middle Kingdom of ancient Egypt (c. 2100 to 1800 B.C.), through the glory days of Alexandria and Pergamum, to the very recent past.[2] In fact, most libraries in the United States today—and this includes thousands of public, school, and other libraries—serve as repositories for artifacts. That libraries are in the process of evolving other functions is certainly relevant to discussion here, but it is also problematic. In the United States schools of library and information science educate individuals to manage complex organizations, to grapple with problems of intellectual and physical access to information, and to incorporate information technology into library service. It remains, however, that most nonlibrarians think of libraries as places where books are stored.

People come by this view of libraries honestly. The early history of libraries provides accounts of collections or conjectures regarding what the collections may have been like. These ancient libraries housed tablets, papyri, and parchment or vellum scrolls. The medium changed slightly in the first centuries A.D., when the codex volume was introduced. The codex slowly gained a foothold as a portable artifact whose properties of retrieval were superior to the scroll. Then in the fifteenth century came the revolutionary technology of printing from movable type. At that point the world changed and—at the risk of reducing such a transforming event to a jejune overstatement—the first information explosion was born. Johann Gensfleisch zum Gutenberg might not have realized what a transcendent change had been wrought, but its effects have been analyzed for popular audiences by James Burke[3] and for scholars by Elizabeth L. Eisenstein.[4]

Before the printing press achieved ascendancy, texts were primarily of an ecclesiastical nature. In fact, clerical dominance continued into the early years of printing. This invention, however, had far too much potential to be of limited use. As Miriam Usher Chrisman points out in her study of the Reformation microcosm of Strasbourg, it was not long before lay culture adopted the printing press for its aims of vernacular publication and the spread of both popular and learned science.[5] The reach of written communication was, during this period, greatly expanded and this, naturally, resulted in what Michael Harris calls "the rapid increase in the size of libraries and a concomitant growth in complexity."[6] Harris writes,

> In a way, the invention of printing may be said to have given birth to modern librarianship, in the sense that the ever-increasing size of library collections made possible by the printing press stimulated the emergence of a profession charged with the responsibility of organizing and directing these at once large, complex, and valuable national resources.[7]

Printing made possible the advent of written communication transmitted via media other than the book. Because the spread of information had become much more rapid, enabling a scientific community to grow and to share discoveries, a new mechanism could arise. Patience with what was perceived by some as the cumbersome, time-consuming book grew thin, and personal correspondence was too limited to be effective on a large scale. Out of this frustration the scientific journal was born. The convenient date of this birth is January 5, 1665—the date of the first issue of the *Journal des scavans*.[8] Scientists and librarians are still feeling the effects of this development.

When Europeans, especially the British, sailed to the New World they carried with them the affinity for print on paper. During the colonial years libraries appeared in many of the newly founded settlements. Some of these had the purpose of seeing to the religious and moral edification of the colonists. Toward that end Thomas Bray, representing the Society for the Promotion of Christian Knowledge, came to America and, in the early eighteenth century, provided for thirty-nine parochial and thirty-five lay libraries.[9] Also in the eighteenth century the social phenomena of the association and "circulating" libraries also had beginnings.[10] By the nineteenth century the United States was ready for the coming of the public library. Through community planning, individual advocacy, and philanthropy the public library has become a public good.

Colonial days also saw the founding of colleges, which were accompanied by libraries. As did the public library, the academic library really began to flourish in the nineteenth century. Westward expansion meant the spread of colleges, in every state and into the territories. As higher education was transformed and universities achieved places of importance in U.S. society and life, libraries became integral to the goals and functions of higher education. Into this century, the presence (and expansion) of universities signaled the growth of library collections. The rate of growth has been traced by Arthur T. Hamlin.[11] Some university libraries have become enormous and have constructed monuments to this enormity in the edifices designed, primarily, to house the collections.

To a lesser degree public libraries have mirrored the growth of academic libraries. Both, however, face the serious problems of space management, publishing output, and economic constriction. A foretaste of the difficulties of libraries was provided in 1944 by Fremont Rider.[12] He examined previous growth patterns of research collections and, by extrapolation, painted a grim picture for librarians. He suggested that, if the growth trend were to continue, the Yale University library of the year 2040 would house 200 million volumes. The reader of today understands that this is an impossibility, but the problem of growth is no less real. And, for all of librarians' rhetoric, numbers continue to play an important part in our lives. We continue to gather and publish library statistics. We still have a tendency to equate quality with quantity. We measure success, in part, by the number of volumes added. It may never be stated, but there is hint of that equation in the gathering of statistics. So, the Association of Research Libraries gathers numbers from its members each year; the Public Library Association, through the Public Library Data Service, counts numbers; the Association of College and Research Libraries periodically publishes data on approximately 3,000 academic libraries collected by the Center for Education Statistics of the U.S. Department of Education. To the governing agencies, these statistics represent means of evaluation and comparison. Even librarians place some faith in the numbers. The epigram to G. Edward Evans's *Developing Library and Information Center Collections* is, "No library of a million volumes can be all bad."[13]

SERVICE IN LIBRARIES

In the last decade-and-a-half a shift has occurred. It is true that libraries have continued to grow in the recent past, but this growth has been the source of a different kind of concern. Self-sufficiency is not only impossible, it is an unrealistic, and perhaps even dangerous, goal. Growth is no longer geometric, as Rider suggested; it is arithmetic. Libraries are adding what approaches a constant number of volumes to their collections each year. As Robert Molyneux cautions, the past is no longer an accurate predictor of the future. More complex phenomena are affecting the growth of libraries; examination of those phenomena may instruct us, not only about growth, but also about the operations of libraries as they exhibit a changing growth model.[14] Furthermore, there is little discernible macroeconomic certainty. Budgets have lost a substantial amount of buying power. Some libraries are bemoaning the price of serials and are retaliating against increases with subscription cancellations. Also, developments in information technology are being incorporated into the storage and retrieval functions of libraries. One result of the problems just enumerated is librarians' heightened awareness of physical limitations of buildings, budgets, and personnel in the face of an information structure that seems to know no such limitations.

One of the responses by librarians to the dilemma of growth has been to emphasize the service aspect of libraries. While libraries have been around a long time, service has not always been an obvious feature of libraries. Of course, making books available to a certain group of people may constitute service, but it is of a quiescent sort. By service I mean here the active participation of a knowledgeable intermediary. Attention to service in libraries coincided, in large part, with the aspiration of librarianship to profession. Initially service manifests itself as assistance to readers, a precursor in many ways to reference service. An early paper stressing the importance of contact with readers was written by Samuel S. Green and published in 1876,[15] the same year the American Library Association was founded and Charles Ammi Cutter published his "Rules for a Dictionary Catalogue." The latter event signified the tide of change in libraries. Not only were patrons being allowed to browse the book stacks in many libraries, but new mechanisms were being designed to give users enhanced access to the holdings of libraries. As we shall see later, these mechanisms, as they have developed over the past century or so, are integral to any examination of communication between library and user. As Michael F. Winter notes, "With the notion of service comes an orientation to the community, of clients as the essential reason for the work in the first place."[16] Winter states that this is one of the hallmarks of professionalism. As librarianship entered the twentieth century, the orientation to community became strengthened and the centrality of communication within this orientation became fixed, if not always conspicuously realized.

In the early writings on assistance to readers and reference there is an implicit recognition that the transaction between patron and librarian constituted a communication process. In 1897 Eleanor B. Woodruff wrote,

> The famous dictum "Speech was given to man to conceal thought," is often forcibly brought to mind by the ingenuity with which visitors to the reference-room suceed in hiding their desires behind their questions. And right here lies the opportunity for the exercise of one of the greatest gifts of the successful librarian—the ability by skillful questioning, without appearance of curiosity or impertinence, to extract from the vaguest, most general requests, a clear idea of what the enquirer really needs.[17]

This excerpt can be seen as a precursor of what would become a burgeoning literature on the reference interview, central to which is an understanding of complex processes of communication. Charles Bunge provides an overview of the history of writing on reference service and the reference interview that is useful both to the student and to the seasoned practitioner.[18]

Down throughout this century other services have been introduced in libraries—some of these have been of a technical nature, others have involved direct contact one person with another. An example of the latter is term paper counseling services offered by some academic libraries. The purpose of such a service is to provide a buffer between the student and the information infrastructure and superstructure. An example of technical change is the online search services offered by most libraries that employ machine-readable databases to handle the storage and retrieval of bibliographic, numeric, and other information. The above services, from the perspective of the user, are locally-based. In a real sense such a service as online searching is not local, since access to a remote database is involved. To the user, though, the remoteness is transparent and the perception is likely to be of one library meeting the needs of an individual. Other services, such as interlibrary loans and cooperative borrowing, are removed from one building, one campus, one community. These kinds of services that transcend the holdings, and even the personnel, of a single library introduce a concept that is not so simple for users to grasp or for libraries to manage. For lack of a better term this concept can be called the metalibrary.[19] This will be examined further in Chapter 4.

INFORMATION THEORY

Investigation into communication at large has its technical side. One of the technical aspects of communications is that of signal transmission. Claude Shannon focused on this in *Mathematical Theory of Communication*. Shannon did not concern himself with content; his province was not meaning. Rather, for Shannon,

> The significant aspect is that the actual message is one selected from a set of possible messages. The system must be designed to operate for each possible selection, not just the one which will actually be chosen since this is unknown at the time of design.
>
> If the number of messages in the set is finite then this number or any monotonic function of this number can be regarded as a measure of the information produced when one message is chosen from the set, all choices being equally likely.[20]

Warren Weaver, in elaborating on Shannon's theory, suggests that, while the theory applies primarily to technical problems of communication—specifically, the accuracy of transmission of symbols—semantic (meaning) problems and effectiveness (influence) problems can be addressed by the theory in a narrow sense (signal accuracy) and in a broader sense because of interrelation of the three levels of problems.[21]

Shannon's ideas can be problematic for anyone approaching the study of communication, because they break with traditional thinking in which a source creates a message and transmits it to a destination. As Seth Finn and Donald F. Roberts point out:

> In contrast to our customary notions about the process of communication, Shannon's theory recognizes that messages themselves do not physically flow from source to destination. Rather the source indicates, by whatever technical means are available, the specific message the destination should select from a set of messages which are held in common at any given moment. This essentially semiotic conceptualization of the communication process is indicated, we believe, in Shannon's illustration of a general communication system. . . . We think it is extremely important to note that the term "message" is confined to the source-transmitter and receiver-destination portions of Shannon's diagram. Only the signal travels between transmitter and receiver.[22]

The "semiotic conceptualization" that Finn and Roberts speak of has special relevance for the kind of communication structure represented by the library. This will be explored later.

The theory of communication set forth by Shannon necessitates a view of information that is quite different from that held by the majority of librarians and information specialists. In dealing with the artifacts collected by libraries we have come to assume that information is represented by discrete sets of data such as tables in a statistical abstract, poems in collection, articles on certain topics, or, in some cases, books. Shannon's notion is distinct from content or meaning. As Weaver notes, "In this new theory the word information relates not so much to what you *do* say, as to what you *could* say. That is, information is a measure of your freedom of choice when you select a message."[23] The degree of choice can be expressed as bits of information. For instance, if one has a choice between two messages, then $\log_2 2 = 1$, so the choice is, since 2 equals 2 to the power of 1, characterized by 1 bit of information. If there is a choice among 256 messages, then there are 8 bits of information, since $\log_2 256 = 8$ since ($256 = 2^8$). Generally, the equation can be expressed as $\log_2 X = N$, where X is the number of messages to choose from and N is the number of bits of information. Further, $X = 2^N$. Shannon refers to "information," or the degree of choice, as entropy, because the mathematical representation of "information" is almost identical to that of entropy, as used in thermodynamics. This representation is

$$H = -\Sigma(p_i \log_2 p_i).$$

This formula is based on probability, so the highest value H can attain is 1, which would signify maximum entropy. If there are two possible choices, then the probability of selecting the first alternative is p_1 and the second is p_2, which is $(1 - p_1)$. In this instance H would equal $-(p_1 \log_2 p_1 + p_2 \log_2 p_2)$. As Weaver points out, "H is largest when the two probabilities are equal (i.e., when one is completely free and unbiased in the choice), and reduces to zero when one's freedom of choice is gone."[24] If entropy, then, is a measure of freedom of choice, then entropy is highest when choice is unfettered, when one option has no better chance of being selected than another. Entropy is also a measure of statistical disorder, so the higher the level of entropy, the more disordered information may be seen to be. If a person is presented with several possible solutions to a problem and has no reason to think that any one is better than the others, then confusion is likely to result. Entropy, or disorder, in such a situation would be high. Information may be limited, but the degree of choice can still be high enough to increase the potential for failed communication.

The above statements may seem a bit arcane, but, in reality, they represent simple concepts.[25] First, we must remember that the logarithm in base 2 of a number is the power to which 2 must be raised to give that number. As was stated earlier, the maximum value of H (maximum entropy) for a pair of choices is 1 and, given two choices, H reaches the maximum when the probabilities of the two choices are equal. A formulaic representation of this equality of choice would be

$$H = -(1/2 \log_2 1/2 + 1/2 \log_2 1/2)$$

Another way of expressing the fraction 1/2 is $1/2^1$ (one over two to the first power), which is the same as 2^{-1}. From this we see that the power to which 2 is raised is –1, so the logarithm of 1/2 is –1. Inserting that value into the formula yields

$$H = -[(1/2)(-1) + (1/2)(-1)]$$
$$H = 1$$

If there were a three-fourths chance of making one choice and a one-fourth chance of making the other, the formula would be

$$H = -(3/4 \log_2 3/4 + 1/4 \log_2 1/4)$$
$$H = -[(3/4)(-.415) + (1/4)(-2)]$$
$$H = .811$$

The value of $\log_2$ of 3/4 is –.415; the value for 1/4 is –2. The resulting computation yields a value for H of .811, which represents a relatively high level of entropy.

Another measure of information is related to entropy and is also important to information theory. That measure is redundancy, and it is a phenomenon that anyone who uses any language should be thankful for. Redundancy enables one person to be understood by another; it makes written and spoken communication possible. If entropy is freedom of choice and is a measure of probability, then redundancy is one minus entropy. Weaver observes that "this fraction of the message is unnecessary in the sense that if it were missing the message would still be essentially complete, or at least it could be completed."[26] Redundancy enables people to save money when sending telegrams, to read letters from friends with bad handwriting, et cetera. The English language is approximately 50 percent redundant, so if a message is missing components, sense may still be made because other components offer a context in which guesses can be made regarding missing words. While entropy represents disorder in that it signifies the degree of choice, redundancy lends order by narrowing choice. For instance, if presented with, "If the cake is done, take it out of the _____," one could easily surmise that the missing word is probably "oven." There may be other possibilities, but one is unlikely to insert "garden" or "dog" into the space.

Any language is a code; a set of statistical rules. In fact, the code is a system that embodies a behavior based on certain probabilities; therefore, it is a stochastic process. More specifically, it is a Markov process—one in which the probability of a future event depends on previous events, especially the immediately previous event. It is possible, furthermore, that the process is ergodic; that is, statistically regular, with any sample representative of the whole. The regularity of this body of statistical rules is largely due to the redundancy and the degree of predictability for which it is responsible. This does not mean the system is simple; redundancy creates an extraordinary array of possibilities for relatedness. However, without redundancy there would be endless choice and, so, a kind of equilibrium or chaos in which choices have equal likelihood of selection at any given time. Redundancy adds constraints to the system so that rules can govern selection. Jeremy Campbell says that is responsible for the path of existence. He says,

> The lesson of information theory is that choice and constraint can coexist as partners, enabling a system, be it a living organism, a language, or a society, to follow the arrow not of entropy but of history. This is the arrow which distinguishes past from future, by moving away from the simple, the uniform and random, and toward the genuinely new, the endlessly complex products of nature and of mind.[27]

These measures present interesting theoretical problems, but what do they hold for any examination of human communication?

In many ways Shannon's work provides a conceptual background upon which further work can build. As Finn and Roberts warn, one does not have to seek precise analogs in human communication for each of Shannon's measures and for each element in his model of communication.[28] Shannon's work can, though, be used as a starting point for modeling the communication process. As to his use of the word "information," Weaver offers an insightful observation:

> One has the vague feeling that information and meaning may prove to be something like a pair of canonically conjugate variables in quantum theory, that is, information and meaning may be subject to some joint restriction that compels the sacrifice of one if you insist in having much of the other.[29]

The concept of information as applied by those interested in information theory (that is, as freedom of choice or a delimiter of uncertainty) is problematic in other ways as well. While Weaver links information and meaning above, the two are certainly not identical and may, furthermore, be epistemologically different. Information, in this narrow sense, is a function of physical capacity—the ability to transmit and receive messages. Meaning, on the other hand, is a function of consciousness. Everett Rogers and D. Lawrence Kincaid write,

> The reduction of uncertainty at the physical level of human information processing . . . has little to do with meaning, which occurs at a higher level of abstraction. The distinction between the physical and the semantic levels of information-processing means that a reduction, and an increase, in uncertainty can occur simultaneously, but at different levels of information processing. Thus, interpreting a particular pattern that one perceives as the word for "Democrat," for example, may reduce one's uncertainty about which word has occurred (the physical level of reality), but at the same time may create uncertainty about the meaning of that particular use of the word "Democrat" (at the psychological level of reality).[30]

The problematic aspects of meaning can provide fodder for further exploration.

COMMUNICATION THEORY

What does it take for one person to be able to communicate with another? One assumption that can be made is that the two individuals should share a common language. If one speaks English and the other Russian, the probability of the one being understood by the other is quite low. Of course, there are ways other than via language to communicate, but the structure, grammar, and syntax of language are designed to enable communication to take place. If the two parties are physically remote—for instance, talking on the telephone or exchanging letters—then language becomes an even more important tool. Harold Lasswell provides a simple description of the act of communication: "Who Says What in Which Channel to Whom with What Effect?"[31] This seemingly innocuous question belies a complex process—one further complicated by interdependence among the stated elements and also the implicit elements of time and situation. Throughout this discourse the factors Lasswell identified will be essential to analysis and discussion.

The importance of language leads Frank Dance to state, "Human communication is the eliciting of a response through verbal symbols."[32] He further elaborates on the "verbal" aspect of communication:

> A verbal symbol can be either vocal or nonvocal. A vocal sound need not always be symbolic. A scream, for instance, may be vocal and nonverbal on the reflex discharge level. On the other hand, a scream, when interpreted by a passerby in terms of circumstances, may be vocal and also may have meaning for the passerby beyond the meaning to the screamer. Thus, the passerby's meaning, being the result of his past actual or vicarious experience, is interpreted by him in terms of words and becomes both vocal and verbal. A traffic signal derives its meaning from the observer's past experiences in learning law and order through words. The traffic signal, then, is nonvocal and verbal. The essential attribute of *verbal* is not the existence of sound in acoustic space, but the representation of abstractions of many instances by one sign that becomes a sign of signs or a symbol. In this light, the use of verbal symbolism many [*sic*] well be redundant; however, we can use it in this early instance to overcome the "noise" of long-standing terminological confusion.[33]

In some cases a shared language is not sufficient for effective communication to take place. Usage of certain words may vary. Does a person from Kansas City know what someone from London means when he refers to the "bonnet" or "boot" of his car? One need not cross an ocean for such obstacles to arise. What would someone from Brooklyn say if someone from Greenville, North Carolina, told him he was going to carry a date to a dance? People from different parts of the country may have sufficiently different referents as to result in a degree of confusion. Likewise, people from different fields of study are likely to have some difficulty communicating. If a physicist mentions a strange attractor to a sociologist, something may be lost in the process. Some professions seem to create their own jargons and, while the purpose of this inside language might not be to exclude those who are not in the know, that might be the effect. Physicians and lawyers have been accused of this kind of seeming obfuscation, but members of the library profession should probably not cast the first stone.

The verbal nature of human communication affects a great deal of human behavior—how we dress, how we spend our time, what jobs we hold, and, to some degree, how we spend our money. David Berlo notes, "There are five verbal communication skills. Two of these are encoding skills: writing and speaking. Two of them are decoding skills: reading and listening. The fifth is crucial to both encoding and decoding: thought or reasoning."[34] As with other skills, these can be improved upon through conscious effort. It is true that, for some people, clear, concise writing or speaking seem natural while others may struggle to produce a brief message. Virtually everyone, however, can enhance these skills with assistance and practice. There is something about our ability to communicate that is basic to our selves, to the way we see the world and our places in it. Limitations to that ability jeopardize an individual's ability to traverse certain realms of society. As Berlo observes,

> our communication skills, our facility in handling the language code, affect our ability to encode thoughts that we have. Our language facility,

our communication ability does more—it actually affects the thoughts themselves. More specifically, the words we can command, and the way that we put them together affect (a) what we think about, (b) how we think, and (c) whether we are thinking at all.[35]

These aspects of communication and its importance to thought affect behavior as well. Since understanding may be impaired, situations in which such an obstacle may occur are likely to be avoided whenever possible. Just as people from different countries who speak different languages might segregate themselves into groups of common backgrounds, so too might people who ostensibly have a shared language. Language may have uses, functions, or purposes apart from communication,[36] but in order for many kinds of communication to take place, language must be employed. Language enables humans to structure thoughts according to rules and conventions (grammar) so that the thoughts may be transmitted from one person to another or may be used internally to relate thought to experience. In the absence of language or its grammar (or the absence of one particular subset of language relevant to a given situation), communication is difficult, if not impossible.

Research in human communication has attempted to address the dynamics of the process in a number of ways. These attempts have been based largely on observations of elements of the process and the roles assumed by people in communication. One difficulty of several efforts is that, in order to observe what is occurring when humans communicate, a sort of snapshot is taken, a still frame of one moment. This may lead to a thorough description of the instant, but may obscure the totality of even a brief exchange. Everett Rogers and D. Lawrence Kincaid take issue with such a seemingly mechanistic view, stating that this research approach has led to seven biases that have hindered the development of theory:

1. A view of communication as a linear, one-way act (usually vertical), rather than a cyclical, two-way process over time.
2. A source bias based on dependency, rather than on the relationship of those who communicate and their fundamental interdependency.

3. A tendency to focus on the objects of communication as simple, isolated physical objects, at the expense of the context in which they exist.
4. A tendency to focus on the messages per se at the expense of silence, and the punctuation and timing of messages.
5. A tendency to consider the primary function of communication to be persuasion, rather than mutual understanding, consensus, and collective action.
6. A tendency to concentrate on the psychological effects of communication on separate individuals, rather than on the social effects and the relationships among individuals within networks.
7. A belief in one-way mechanistic causation, rather than mutual causation that characterizes human information systems that are fundamentally cybernetic.[37]

Both the traditional approach to communication and the departure advocated by Rogers and Kincaid (and others) have led to efforts aimed at modeling communication. Models may provide a clearer, more understandable, picture of the process; some of them will be helpful in examining the library environment.

Despite some of the problems of communication, humans are driven to communicate, and the purposes or objectives of communication vary over time for any individual and among individuals at any given time. During an exchange between two people, one is likely to be in the role of sender and the other of receiver. Wilbur Schramm creates a simple table to represent these roles in the process.

from the *sender's* viewpoint	**from the *receiver's* viewpoint**
the objective of communication may be to:	
1. Inform	1. Understand
2. Teach	2. Learn
3. Please	3. Enjoy
4. Propose or persuade	4. Dispose or decide[38]

Of course, this oversimplifies a process that is in constant flux, with one objective yielding to another or objectives interweaving in a complex matrix of purpose. Nonetheless, this table provides a glimpse of possibilities during a brief moment in time.

To complicate matters further, communication may have individual and social objectives. Schramm attempts to depict this as well:

viewed *socially*	**viewed *individually***
the objective of communication may be to:	
1. Share common knowledge of environment	1. Test or expand picture of reality, learn of opportunities and dangers
2. Socialize new members of society to play their roles and abide by norms and customs	2. Acquire skills and knowledge necessary to live comfortably in society
3. Entertain members, distract them from troubles and dissatisfactions, create artistic form	3. Enjoy, relax, sometimes escape from real problems, sometimes gain oblique insight into them
4. Gain working consensus on policy, win allies or followers, control behavior and disperse resources in desired direction	4. Reach decisions where choice available, take action on informed basis, behave in socially desirable way[39]

Again, it is often difficult to separate these items into discrete, singly-occuring phenomena. It may be more useful to view these elements as being in motion, shifting from individual to social and back again, attaching themselves to one another as atoms do to form molecules, flowing at varying speeds depending on the situation. The motion may even appear random, but it is directly related to the states of each individual's consciousness *and* to group dynamics.

Finally, for now, there are some qualities or aspects of communication that should be taken into account here. Communication, as an entity or a process or a system, is a phenomenon central to human culture, existence, and activity. With this in mind, E. L. Cerroni-Long enumerates several features of communication that need to be kept in mind throughout this discourse.[40]

1. Communication is continuous. Thus, a description of culture that focuses on events chosen "for their relevance" by the observer is not reliable from a communicative point of view. Absence of "relevant action" should be taken into serious account (and recorded) since it serves to transfer information just as much as "events" do.
2. Communication is unrepeatable; that is, it operates within a discretionary (rather than deterministic) system. In such a system input cannot be determined by identification of output and a model of action has to be based on probabilistic rather than mechanistic premises.
3. Communication is irreversible, which adds to the previous axiom by indicating the factor of direction.
4. Communication is dynamic; that is, highly "circumstantial."
5. Communication is of two types: digital and analogical. Very often the two are mixed, as in the use of non-verbal behavior (analogical communication) while talking (digital communication).
6. Human interaction (interpersonal communication) is always either complementary or symmetrical. Also, it is always organized in sequences of interchanges, the punctuation of which should be identified and analyzed. However, the sequences are affected by feedback, thus a cybernetic, rather than structural approach, should be used in analyzing them.

In the remaining chapters we will explore how this complex process of communication is a part of everything inherent in a library. We could explore other aspects of the phenomenon, such as organizational communication, but others have already tackled some of these problems.[41] Rather, the focus will be on communication as it affects the user of the library. This necessitates looking at the stuff that goes into libraries, both artifacts and access. As an aid to conceptualization, models of communication will be presented as they have relevance to the topic at hand. Both the library and the librarians will be examined to see how the process can be facilitated and how it sometimes is short-circuited. Lastly, those disruptive forces (human, technical, and other) that act to subvert the best of intentions will be investigated.

NOTES

1. Arthur Curley and Dorothy Broderick, *Building Library Collections*, 6th ed. (Metuchen, NJ: Scarecrow Press, 1985), 1.
2. Sidney L. Jackson, *Libraries and Librarianship in the West: A Brief History* (New York: McGraw-Hill, 1974).
3. James Burke, *The Day the Universe Changed* (Boston: Little, Brown and Co., 1985), 111–23.
4. Elizabeth L. Eisenstein, *The Printing Press as an Agent of Change: Communications and Cultural Transformations in Early-Modern Europe*, vols. I and II (Cambridge, England: Cambridge University Press, 1979).
5. Miriam Usher Chrisman, *Lay Culture, Learned Culture: Books and Social Change in Strasbourg, 1480–1599* (New Haven, CT: Yale University Press, 1982).
6. Michael H. Harris, *History of Libraries in the Western World*, compact textbook ed. (Metuchen, NJ: Scarecrow Press, 1984), 117.
7. Ibid.
8. Bernard Houghton, *Scientific Periodicals: Their Historical Development, Characteristics and Control* (Hamden, CT: Linnet Books and Clive Bingley, 1975), 13.
9. Charles T. Laugher, *Thomas Bray's Grand Design: Libraries of the Church of England in America, 1695–1785* (Chicago: American Library Association, 1973).
10. Jesse H. Shera, *Introduction to Library Science: Basic Elements of Library Service* (Littleton, Colo.: Libraries Unlimited, 1976), 35–36.
11. Arthur T. Hamlin, *The University Library in the United States: Its Origins and Development* (Philadelphia: University of Pennsylvania Press, 1981), 232–37.
12. Fremont Rider, *The Scholar and the Future of the Research Library: A Problem and Its Solution* (New York: Hadham Press, 1944).
13. G. Edward Evans, *Developing Library and Information Center Collections*, 2nd ed. (Littleton, CO: Libraries Unlimited, 1987).
14. Robert E. Molyneux, "Patterns, Processes of Growth, and the Projection of Library Size: A Critical Review of the Literature on Academic Library Growth," *Library & Information Science Research*, 8 (January–March 1986), 26–27.

15. Samuel S. Green, "Personal Relations Between Librarians and Readers," *Library Journal*, 1 (October 1876), 74–81.

16. Michael F. Winter, *The Culture and Control of Expertise: Toward a Sociological Understanding of Librarianship* (Westport, CT: Greenwood Press, 1988), p. 117.

17. Eleanaor B. Woodruff, "Reference Work," *Library Journal*, 22 (Conference Issue 1897), 65–67.

18. Charles A. Bunge, "Interpersonal Dimensions of the Reference Interview: A Historical Review of the Literature," *Drexel Library Quarterly*, 20 (Spring 1984), 4–23.

19. I have to confess a prejudice against such terminology, except when used in jest, as James Gleick does when he writes, "The pen line, though hard to read, developed a wobble on top of a wobble—a metawobble," in *Chaos: Making a New Science* (New York: Viking, 1987), 205. Nonetheless, the meta- prefix is descriptive of the transcendent aspect of an entity providing information about information.

20. Claude E. Shannon and Warren Weaver, *The Mathematical Theory of Communication* (Urbana: University of Illinois Press, 1949), 31–32.

21. Ibid., 4.

22. Seth Finn and Donald F. Roberts, "Source, Destination, and Entropy: Reassessing the Role of Information Theory in Communication Research," *Communication Research*, 11 (October 1984), 456.

23. Warren Weaver, "The Mathematics of Communication," *Scientific American*, 181 (July 1949), 12.

24. Shannon and Weaver, *The Mathematical Theory of Communication*, 15.

25. John R. Pierce, *An Introduction to Information Theory: Symbols, Signals & Noise*, 2nd ed. (New York: Dover Publications, Inc., 1980), 81–84.

26. Weaver, "The Mathematics of Communication," 13.

27. Jeremy Campbell, *Grammatical Man: Information, Entropy, Language, and Life* (New York: Simon & Schuster, 1982), 265.

28. Finn and Roberts, "Source, Destination, and Entropy," 453–76.

29. Weaver, "The Mathematics of Communication," 13.

30. Everett M. Rogers and D. Lawrence Kincaid, *Communication Networks: Toward a New Paradigm for Research* (New York: Free Press, 1983), 54–55.

31. Harold D. Lasswell, "The Structure and Function of Communication in Society," in *The Communication of Ideas*, ed. Lyman Bryson (New York: Harper & Row, 1948), 37.

32. Frank E. X. Dance, "Toward a Theory of Human Communication," in *Human Communication: Original Essays* (New York: Holt, Rinehart and Winston, 1967), 289.

33. Ibid., 290.

34. David K. Berlo, *The Process of Communication: An Introduction to Theory and Practice* (New York: Holt, Rinehart and Winston, 1960), 41–42.
35. Ibid., 43.
36. Noam Chomsky, *Reflections on Language* (New York: Pantheon Books, 1975).
37. Rogers and Kincaid, *Communication Networks: Toward a New Paradigm for Research*, 38–39.
38. Wilbur Schramm, "The Nature of Communication Between Humans," in *The Process and Effects of Mass Communication*, ed. Wilbur Schramm and Donald F. Roberts, rev. ed. (Urbana: University of Illinois Press, 1971), 19.
39. Ibid., 20.
40. E. L. Cerroni-Long, "Culture as Communication: Defining the Parameters of Analysis," *Communication & Cognition*, 18 (1985), 385–86.
41. Norman D. Stevens, *Communication Throughout Libraries* (Metuchen, NJ: Scarecrow Press, 1983).

2

Libraries, Information, and Meaning

A REASON FOR BEING

Why libraries? This question is not meant to be facetious. It is one in a series of questions relating to the topic of this book. One of the first is: What is communicated in the communication process? One response to the question might be: Information. This seems to be an unsatisfactory answer, but a more satisfactory one is elusive. One major reason for the dissatisfaction is the lack of a usable, reasonable definition of information. Defining information is key to further discussion, but will be postponed until we consider the original question.

"Why libraries?" is asked in the context of use of libraries. In other words, what in libraries do users find useful? What attracts people to libraries? What benefits do people derive from libraries? What is the library's product? At the risk of initiating an endless do-loop, the response to the last question can be—Information. This may also seem to the reader to be overly simplistic; as we will see, this answer is every bit as complex as the definition of information itself. Many libraries have "information" desks, "information" hotlines, "information" services. At the same time, the typical shopping mall has an "Information" desk. It would not be fruitful, though, for a shopper to approach such a desk and ask something like: "How do you caponize a chicken?" or: "What's the title of the poem that's inscribed on the Statue of Liberty?" Clearly there are different operational definitions of information at work.

Some brave souls who have ventured definitions of information see it as a step in a hierarchy that has data as its lowest level. P. Dorn stated, "Data is the ore, the raw material from which information is developed."[1] In a similar vein F. Keay noted that "data are first condensed into information and from this information meaning is distilled."[2] Others have attached the concept of meaning to information; this is problematic since "information" itself is not inherently meaningful. This will be discussed further. The hierarchy begins with data at the bottom, moves up to information, then to knowledge, and ultimately to wisdom. It would be the rare library that would have the capability of dispensing wisdom to users, but it may be possible that an individual comes to wisdom with some assistance from the content of artifacts in libraries. An argument has been made that the vast majority of libraries are, at their essence, educational institutions. The purpose of education is to transcend information and to achieve the transfer of knowledge.

If we turn to a dictionary definition of information we are struck by the paradox of what has been variously taken as process, commodity, industry, or, as R. K. Stamper observes of past usage, mystical fluid.[3] *Webster's Third New International Dictionary* offers one definition: "the communication or reception of knowledge or intelligence." The example attached to this definition is "the function of a public library is [information]." Another definition, however, is, "facts and figures ready for communication or use as distinguished from those incorporated in a formally organized branch of knowledge." It seems as though the second definition more closely approaches common usage today. This usage creates some problems for anyone who speaks of an "information" service, such as that provided by a library. Pauline Wilson, in examining the purpose of an academic library, states,

> Another notion is that information must reduce uncertainty. Again, simple reflection will show that notion to be incorrect; in fact, some information increases uncertainty. Another qualifying characteristic sometimes attached to information is that is must be useful or valuable. Another is that it must be correct. Both notions are wrong. The world is full of useless and incorrect information. Useless and incorrect as it may be it remains information.[4]

In her discourse on what information is not, Wilson takes issue with Fritz Machlup and accepts a broad definition of the word, as is evident from the passage above.[5]

The difficulty with a definition of information may seem to be a trivial problem, but it is actually central to the business of libraries. When it is said that libraries acquire, store, and retrieve information it is frequently more proper to replace "information" with "data," because "data" seems to be more descriptive of the value-neutral, commodity-driven aspect of the "information industry." In narrow terms, a library user frequently wades through data, seeking that which informs, that which gives significance. In doing so, the user dismisses some data in order to get to information. The average annual rainfall in a portion of Botswana is mere data to many people, a statistic without a context, but to someone studying the connections among climate, agriculture, and economy of southern Africa, it is information. The distinction is important. Donald MacKay defines information as "that which enables us to make a selection from a set of possibilities about which we are ignorant."[6] By this narrow definition information *does* reduce uncertainty, *is* useful, and *is* correct. In this sense there is no such thing as bad information; there either is information or there is not. In this sense, misinformation is an unfortunately misleading word, unless it is taken narrowly to mean the opposite of information.

Christopher John Fox, in his examination of the broad scope of this problem, concludes that informing does not require an inherent truth, but that misinforming requires falsity.[7] This sheds a bit more light on the distinction between the two terms and concepts, but does not go as far as the narrow definition applied here. Misinformation here is not a kind of information; it has a different nature and has a different effect on the receiver of communication. This does not stop us from speaking of people having bad or unreliable information. As Fred Dretske observes, however, false information and misinformation are not varieties of information "any more than decoy ducks and rubber ducks are kinds of ducks."[8] A library builds a collection with the intention of informing. It is intended to be used in a context that is, at its basis, established by the user.

This last statement needs some elaboration. It should be added that, for a successful information exchange, the context is established by the user. For example, if a high school or college student enters a library to write a paper on, say, *The Great Gatsby*, without having read the novel and without having formulated an approach to the assignment, the probability of success is low. The student is likely to be met with data from which no meaning can be inferred. Generally speaking, information is a component that can be added to an individual's knowledge base. A person without a background in science would not be informed by being told that a neutrino is a kind of lepton with no electric charge and probably no mass. The knowledge base likely does not exist to give that datum a context.

Wilson makes a salient point when she writes,

> Information is acquired by being told. Knowledge can be acquired by thinking. Information is a process. Knowledge is a state. Information is a flow of messages. Knowledge is a stock. Information is bit and pieces of discrete information [witness the problem of technology], fragmented and particular. Knowledge is coherent and structured, it often has enduring value.[9]

Information does not produce knowledge; its presence does not necessarily lead to new knowledge. Knowledge may be increased, however, by the assimilation of information, by the structuring of information into something meaningful. A theme running throughout Theodore Roszak's *The Cult of Information* is that the mind thinks with ideas, not with information.[10] This is an important distinction, one that librarians should remind themselves of frequently.

It is difficult, then, to make the claim that libraries are in a knowledge industry. In fact, it is difficult to imagine a "knowledge industry" at all. As is implicit in the passage by Wilson, knowledge is not structured or defined by one person for another. One individual may foster the acquisition of knowledge, may facilitate its development, but knowledge, unlike information, cannot be transmitted. Knowledge, also, is not incremental in the same ways that data and information are. It is not increased in quantities as neatly measurable as bytes or even books. It is a linear phenomenon. Thought on knowledge acquisition may be able to borrow eventually from chaos theory. While a person may use a library to facilitate the acquisition of knowledge, that person does not acquire knowledge from the library.

It is reasonable to say that libraries are a part of the information industry. Libraries may be, along with education, the essential components of the information industry. The act of informing implies mediation between mere data and the receiver; the structure of libraries includes the centrality of mediation. This phenomenon is part of the selection process in libraries; items are acquired that have potential value to the library's community. In the terminology of mechanics, the library's collection, available for use but not yet used, represents potential energy. Through use it is informed into kinetic energy. Cataloging exists to provide structured access to the data in a library. Reference service takes this concept a step further to provide active mediation at the time of expressed need. Successful library use equates with informing.

This discourse suggests that libraries (and other organizations) may be on the wrong track when they speak of information as a commodity. Harlan Cleveland points out that the management concepts that have been developed to deal with *things* present a set of inoperable assumptions when dealing with *information* (that is, symbols or signs).[11] To borrow one of Thomas Kuhn's constructs for paradigms, what we now need is a paradigm shift.[12] If libraries are not traders in a commodity (such as timber, oil, and steel) and they are not creators or storehouses of knowledge, then what model fits the library approaching the twenty-first century? The tendency of librarians has been to think of information in terms of the container—the book, the video, the disk—rather than the content. Reference librarians would argue with this statement on the grounds that the reference function has provided mediation between the information producer and the information user. While this has been an ostensible activity in libraries, the process has been largely value-neutral and noninterpretive. Librarians have frequently aimed to bring together the physical item and the user and then to stand aside. Such an approach ignores the realization that the physical item is not the same as its content and that each user will absorb and interpret that content differently. Catalogers would argue with the above statement on the grounds that the purpose of cataloging is to enhance access and that can only be accomplished by the intellectual process of identifying the subject content of the work and classifying it among like content. This is the intent of cataloging and classification, but success is limited by a practice that limits one physical item to one classification and a complex set of ideas to perhaps two subject headings. It becomes evident that the operative functioning of a library is, from a managerial and even a tacit intellectual point of view, introverted, or inward-looking. If we take paradigm to be that set of shared beliefs and activities of a field or discipline, then here we have the manifest paradigm of librarianship. This is a large and important issue and should be discussed at much greater length, but the treatment here will focus on the antithesis of the dominant behavior—an extroverted, or externally-oriented view of the communication purpose inherent and explicit in libraries.

Perhaps a reasonable suggestion for the focus of examination in the future is concentration on the connection between libraries and semiotics. This may seem to reach far afield, but it is important to remember the essential role the communication process plays in semiotics. Umberto Eco, author of *The Name of the Rose*, studied language and semiotics. He states the following regarding communication and signification:

> When the destination [of a signal] is a human being, or "addressee" (it is not necessary that the source or the transmitter be human, provided that they emit the signal following a system of rules known by the human addressee), we are on the contrary witnessing a process of signification—provided that the signal is not merely a stimulus but arouses an interpretive response in the addressee. This process is made possible by the existence of a code.
>
> A code is a system of signification, insofar as it couples present entities with absent units. When—on the basis of an underlying rule—something actually presented to the perception of the addressee *stands for* [emphasis in original] something else, there is *signification*. In this sense the addressee's actual perception and interpretive behavior are not necessary for the definition of a significant relationship as such; it is enough that the code should foresee an established correspondence between that which "*stands for*" and its correlate, valid for every possible addressee even if no addressee exists or ever will exist.
>
> A signification system is an autonomous semiotic construct that has an abstract mode of existence independent of any possible communicative act it makes possible. On the contrary (except for stimulation process) *every act of communication to or between human beings*—or any other intelligent biological or mechanical apparatus—*presupposes a signification system as its necessary condition.*[13]

Part of this connection between libraries and semiotics includes semantical and syntactical aspects. A system, such as a library, creates or adapts sets of rules to govern relations between expression and their designata; that is, there is an underlying syntax that can be applied to the use of symbols for more concrete things. A library's classification scheme can be seen as a portion of its syntactical structure, as can cataloging rules and even the physical structure (assuming that structure is based somehow on division by content). Semiotics, though, combines these syntactical and semantical aspects with what Walker Percy calls behavioristics, "in which organisms are studied in their relation to their environment as it is mediated by signs."[14] (As Eco is a student of language who has written fiction, Percy is a novelist who has studied language.) It is this latter concept of behavioristics that may have special relevance to the way libraries work, since libraries are nothing without users and use necessitates a process of communication.

Percy notes the utility of using Charles Peirce's meaning triad as a way of understanding semiotics (see Figure 2.1).[15] The sign in the triad "has direction relation of designation with the object, precisely insofar as it is specified by a semantical rule to designate the object. Syntactics has to do with the logical relation which one sign bears to another."[16] With regard to libraries, this is a complex but illustrative construct. An example of this usage of sign may be a classification number, which designates an object—say, a book. The book, further, is a sign or set of signs, designating a different sort of object—ideas. For that matter, each datum within a library's collection is a sign designating some object, which may be an idea or a more tangible or concrete object. It is important to keep in mind that the sign functions, not necessarily as a representation of the object itself or of its being, but often as a representation of the concept of the object, including what the object may connote.

Figure 2.1
Peirce's Meaning Triad

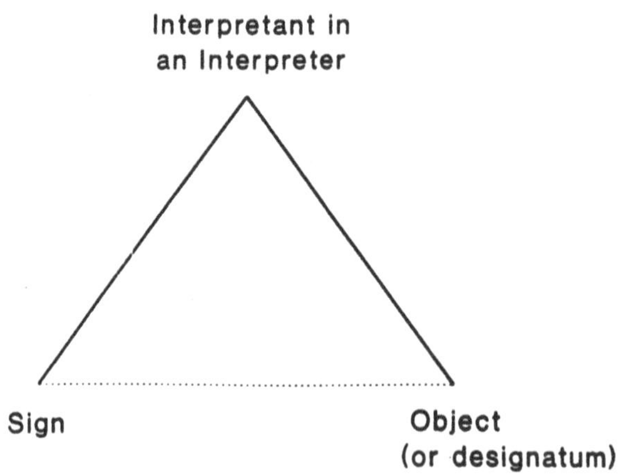

Source: Walker Percy, *The Message in the Bottle* (New York: Farrar, Straus and Giroux, 1975): 246. Reprinted with permission of the publisher.

The third element of the triad, the interpretant, is essential in relating the sign to the object. It is possible that, because of differences in interpretants, a given sign may have different designata for different individuals. The interpretant is, at its core, the tools (thoughts, concepts, contexts) used by an organism for the purpose of interpreting. If the organism lacks sufficient tools there may be a breakdown in this system. Elements in a library, other than those that form its semantical or syntactical base, may be used by an individual (organism) to generate new interpretants. These elements, which may themselves be signs, take advantage of existing interpretants (i.e., thoughts or contexts) to facilitate the connection between sign and object. The elements may take the physical forms of printed or online guides to the library or human intervention by the library personnel.

Eco states that "the sign is an instruction for interpretation, a mechanism which starts from an initial stimulus and leads to all its illative [inferential] consequences."[17] When this is part of a conscious communication process (communication with a purpose, as it were), there is the possibility of something other than success. As is noted above, the library operates according to a set of syntactical and semantical rules, as does a language. If an organism is not familiar with the rules, the organism will likely not be able to incorporate interpretants that are useful for connecting sign with object. An analogy with language can be drawn. If a person does not speak "library," how much does that person need to know to get by? In the case of infrequent or casual use, the equivalent of a phrasebook may suffice. For complex or frequent use, however, that person may need to learn the "grammar" and "vocabulary" of the library.

This semiotic approach may provide a map for examining the subsurface structures of library operations. Maybe there is less than optimal use of libraries in part because the language of the library is not transparent to the user. In order to insure greater success of libraries, we must be more aware that the structure of libraries exists and that its elements may not be widely shared by the populace. These semiotic principles will enter into further discussion of the library and the librarian in the communication process.

INFORMATION AND MEANING

Distinction Between the Two

A further difficulty arises in the discourse on information when the concept of meaning enters the picture. Although the first section of this chapter offered a particular definition of information—one based on contextual significance and a reduction of uncertainty—the customary definition of information used in libraries corresponds more closely with data. Using that popular definition emphasizes the distinctions between information and meaning. The primary point relevant to the difference is that information has no inherent meaning. Meaning in this sense is analogous to knowledge in that it resides in the mind of the individual, rather than in the fact or datum. The problem is complicated, though, because both the sender and the receiver of a message have a conception of meaning, but the two conceptions may not be in agreement.

Part of the problem of this aspect of the communication process, as Weaver observes, is semantic. Difficulty may be evident because of lack of consonance between "the interpretation of meaning by the receiver, as compared with the intended meaning of the sender."[18] The act of communication itself does not involve the transmission of meaning, but, more simply, the transmission of a message. The meaning of the message is implied by the sender and inferred by the receiver. Success of communication depends on transmitting a message in such a way as to produce agreement between inference and implication. There are numerous potential pitfalls in this relationship. As Colin Cherry notes, "The writer or speaker does not communicate his *thoughts* [emphasis Cherry's] to us; he communicates a representation for carrying out this function, under the severe discipline of using the only materials he has, sound and gesture."[19]

It is tempting to think of meaning as something fixed, something static. Such a notion may arise as a part of Western culture based largely on Christian beliefs. Most Western people have been raised to think that Scripture, for instance, has a clear meaning and that meaning has been passed down by generations of clergy. Even in this realm of supposed fixity of meaning, some important questions inevitably assert themselves. If Scripture has but one meaning, why is there not one Christian church; why do numerous sects exist? Even within sects, why is there disagreement among theologians? Why has there been a preponderance of exegetical writings seeking the meaning behind Scripture? Why is there disagreement about the very content of Scripture? These are questions that plague many thoughtful individuals about an area of their lives where there was once a degree of certainty. Imagine the uncertainty surrounding the many daily communications that are not tied to faith.

The realization dawns that meaning is a dependent, and possibly even a transitory, phenomenon. David Berlo recognizes that there are some essential implications that go along with the concept of meaning.[20] First, a message received acts as an internal stimulus and results in an internal response on the part of the receiver. Second, both internal factors and external forces may affect the receiver's inference on meaning. Third, in order for meaning to be inferred from message, the receiver must share some points of reference with the sender. Fourth, the passage of time and the accumulation of experience and other stimuli may contribute to changed inferences of meaning. Finally, meaning is not spatially fixed; when a message is received by more than one person, the possibilities for uniquely inferred meanings (to a degree) increase as the number of receivers increases. Berlo further states, "Communication does not consist of the transmission of meaning. Meaning is not transmittable, not transferable. Only messages are transmittable, and meanings are not in the message, they are in the message-users."[21]

Berlo's points are integral to an understanding of meaning itself, but they also have particular relevance to the topic at hand—communication in libraries. First, a library user does not approach a library as a blank slate. The user's interaction with the library and librarians triggers thought, opinion, possibly even prejudice within the user. That person will formulate meaning based on past experience, hearsay, and exposure to imagery that may include stereotype. A person who is left-brain dominant may approach the library from a primarily logical perspective, focusing on information storage and retrieval. A right-brain dominant person may respond to the library on the basis of aesthetic or other, less rational, responses. Librarians must be aware that, once an individual enters the library, it is probably too late to alter internal responses entirely. Such a transformation would require as much time as it takes to discard stereotypes and preconceptions.

Berlo's second observation should be familiar to every reader: meaning is affected by how the message is received. A library building that is logically arranged, that makes instinctual sense to the user, is likely to produce a stimulus that will enhance the formation of meaning, that will create a receptivity. The first message transmitted to a library user is not apt to emanate from a human, but from the library itself. Further, that initial message may influence the reception of future messages. Librarians are cognizant of user responses to the services of libraries. Library education, in-service training, and performance evaluation all stress the importance of the librarian–user dialogue. By the time a user reaches the librarian, however, that person, has been influenced by stimuli such as the library's physical structure, and has responded in some way to each. This is especially important when we consider that many (if not most) library users interact only with the physical facility. If these responses are negative, the librarian faces an uphill battle in shifting the response mode of the user.

The third point may be the most important. Its import is clearly evident at a superficial level: if one person speaks to another in Russian, but the second understands no Russian, there will be no language communication. The postulate has subtleties beyond such a gross example, though. In one sense, to harken back to Weaver once again, there may be the dilemma of semantics. Certain words or constructions may carry no meaning for a library user. What is more likely, usage varies from librarian to user. For instance, a reference librarian may imply one thing when telling the user to consult an index (a bibliographic tool that analyzes—by name, title, subject or other field—documents) while the user infers something else from the word "index" (a finding aid at the back of a book). This example illustrates that language is more than merely a particular dialect; within a given language there are many possibilities for meaning. We may speak the "language" of libraries (or of law, or medicine or business). If the receiver is not fluent in that language, communication is much more difficult.

The importance of language cannot be understated. C. K. Ogden and I. A. Richards begin their treatise on meaning with an acknowledgment of the link between language and thought.[22] To illustrate, try to think of something, anything, without incorporating language into the thought. It is extremely difficult to envision discretely graphic thought; not that is is impossible for everyone. But even those graphic images are likely to be accompanied by the structure of language. This is not meant to imply that people think solely by means of language, but it is extremely difficult to separate thought and language. Not only would the separation be difficult, but the dependence of one on the other signifies a delimitation that defines the universe of potential thought for an individual. As Berlo writes,

> our communication skills, our facility in handling the language code, affects our ability to encode thoughts that we have. Our language facility, our communication ability does more—it actually affects the thoughts themselves. More specifically, the words we can command, and the way that we put them together affect (a) what we think about, (b) how we think, and (c) whether we are thinking at all.[23]

A shared language increases the likelihood of sharing thought, which, in turn, increases the likelihood of agreement between implied and inferred meaning. Paul Watzlawick and others write, "While it is perfectly possible to transmit strings of symbols with syntactical accuracy, they would remain meaningless unless sender and receiver had agreed beforehand on their significance."[24] This echoes, in part, the discussion of semiotics above and illustrates the connection between a semiotic approach to communication and the concept of meaning. The interpreter of any sign must have a working interpretant (a thought or idea) that can help infer meaning from the sign. The sign, however (and language comes under the rubric of "sign"), may be correct, but the correctness may depend upon context. Communication succeeds more often when the context is understood and accepted by all parties to the process. This is why metaphors, especially similes, are effective in poetry and education; the use of language can create a common context to foster understanding.

The final two of Berlo's points are self-evident, especially in light of the preceding discussion. To use a library example to illustrate the fourth implication, the same type of library service is not likely to be effective for both children and adults. The adult has more experience that is likely to be relevant to the use of a library—a longer exposure to various media, a more extensive educational background, a broader experience with differing communication circumstances. The assumptions made in providing service to the one are probably not going to be safe for the other. In the same way that a person changes over time, a society or culture changes. The change may be reflected in behavior or in language; in either case, what once was inferred may be inferred no longer. To some school children, reading Shakespeare is akin to reading a foreign language; the interpretants are not equipped to make sense of the sign. More subtle changes in recent years may be altering inferences made by large segments of society. For instance, a virtual generation of investors and stockbrokers may have difficulty finding meaning in a Dow-Jones industrial average of 800.

Just as there are diachronous variations in meaning formation (changes over time), there may be synchronous variations as well (differences at one point in time among a number of individuals or groups exposed to the same message). One reason for this is the lack of uniformity of language facility. It is unrealistic and unproductive to assume that a message from a single source aimed at several receivers simultaneously will have the same effect on each receiver. For instance, children learn by different means;

some use auditory means, some are more sensitive to visual stimuli, some are best reached by tactile means. What this portends is that things can go awry in the communication process.

Dysfunctions

Human communication of any sort is, to some degree, a thing of chance. Success depends upon a number of variables, many of which are beyond the control of the sender or the receiver. As is noted in the introductory chapter, if two individuals speak different languages, the odds of success are small. As is also noted, two speakers of English may fail to understand one another if they do not share an operational language, such as that of law, medicine, or librarianship. Information theory is constructed to recognize the necessity of some degree of sharing of a system of symbols. Willis Jackson observed almost forty years ago:

> Incomplete knowledge of the future, and also of the past of the transmitter from which the future might be constructed, is at the very basis of the concept of information. On the other hand complete ignorance also precludes communication; a common language is required, that is to say an agreement between the transmitter and the receiver regarding the elements used in the communication process. . . . the information of a message can be defined as the "minimum number of binary decisions which enable the receiver to reconstruct the message, on the basis of the data already available to him." These data comprise both the convention regarding the symbols and the language used, and the knowledge available at the moment when the message started.[25]

It becomes evident that, while we take for granted our ability to communicate, there are obstacles standing in the way of success. Common language also takes on new meaning when we contemplate how specialized our society has become. People engaged in the same line of work may have difficulty communicating if their specializations do not mesh. The presence of potential obstacles could lead us to wonder how communication takes place at all. Niklas Luhmann has articulated this doubt:

> Immediately, it becomes evident that a multitude of problems and obstacles have to be surmounted before communication can come about. The first improbability is that, given the separateness and individuality of human consciousness, one person can understand what another means. ... The second improbability relates to the research of recipients. It is improbable that a communication should reach more persons than are present in a given situation..... The third improbability is the improbability of success. Even if a communication is understood, there can be no assurance of its being accepted.... These improbabilities are not only obstacles preventing a communication from reaching its target; they also function as thresholds of discouragement and lead to abstention from communication if the prospects for it are thought to be inauspicious.[26]

The obstacles are manifest as individual, social, and technical phenomena. The primary importance of Luhmann's observations may be that communication is not haphazard (or at least is not successful if haphazard) and cannot be left to chance. It requires conscious and directed effort to succeed. The question implicit in this is how much effort are people willing to exert and how much is the return going to be on their effort. In economic terms there needs to be at least a quid pro quo so that an individual does not believe that effort exceeds return. This is true of the library as well. We should ask: Is the library easy to use? Does it require a great deal of effort on the part of the user? Is that potential expenditure of effort keeping people away from the library? It is axiomatic that one way to reduce demand for something is to make it difficult to use. If the library is difficult to use, is that intentional on the part of librarians? Do we create a situation in which failure is more probable? Recognition of the potential for failure may be one means of ensuring success.

Obstacles to communication are certainly obstacles to meaning formation as well. This has societal and individual implications. As Orrin Klapp states, "In a crisis of meaning, people find much that doesn't make sense, little that is basic or reliable to hang onto."[27] This "meaning lag" that may be large-scale affliction could be reflected in a dichotomy between information and meaning. Information here is used in the sense applicable to information theory—degree of choice. Klapp further offers the possibility that

> the lag from which society suffers be expressed as relationship not between material and nonmaterial culture but between different sorts of information: on the one hand, mere information conceived as reduction of uncertainty in any binary (yes-or-no) choice, commonly measured in bits; and, on the other, meaning as information about the relation of something to a pattern or scheme of which one is part—an awareness that is necessarily subjective.[28]

Effort at enhancing meaning formation by increasing the transmission of information may, then, be counterproductive. Too much information can result in overload and may become a source of noise. It is not that information and meaning are unrelated—there must be a stimulus if there is to be a response—but the relationship is not necessarily direct or proportional. Is this true of the library also? Does it bombard the user with stimuli to the point that the response is avoidance? The relationship may be founded on Weaver's suggestion: "One has the vague feeling that information and meaning may prove to be something like a pair of canonically conjugate variables in quantum theory, that is, that information and meaning may be subject to some joint restriction that compels the sacrifice of one if you insist on having much of the other."[29]

Inference of meaning is particularly elusive for the reasons outlined above and for other, very basic, reasons. As Watzlawick and others note, sender and receiver must agree on the significance of the symbols. This harkens back to the semiotic properties of communications. Language, being a code based on specific signs, is at least somewhat ambiguous. Signs may be interpreted differently, depending upon context, referents, and the knowledge possessed by the sender and the receiver. To librarians who have been sensitized by education and experience, certain signs (words, phrases, etc.) signify specific things. The meaning inferred from such signs is thus in keeping with the signification, just as experienced drivers infer meaning from road signs and understand

"Stop" and "Yield." An individual who knows how to drive, but who has never seen a "Yield" sign, for example, may not necessarily behave in the manner expected by other drivers. International road symbols constitute an effort to unify implied and inferred meaning by finding common signs—signs that should elicit more uniform inferences—based, not on language, but on graphic symbols.

The stimulus-response concept inherent in Berlo's first two implications of communication are dependent upon signification. The sign embodies both an internal and an external stimulus; the response follows both of these stimuli. It is important to remember, though, that signs are not isolated, they do not occur in a strictly linear fashion, and they do not always wait for a response. Paul Kecskemeti observes,

> To say that sign S has meaning is to say that *when* S is present, the response R is "good" in terms of some standard; to say that the organism O "interprets" S in terms of this meaning is to say that for O the situation will be structured around the possibility of the "good" result that may be attained by performing R. How O will actually respond depends on many factors; for instance, the "good" response may be inhibited by some other sign S′, whose interpretation will cancel the seeking of the goal toward which R is oriented.[30]

Conflicting or ambiguous signs may result in confusion or false communication (a sense that the exchange is successful when implication and interference are actually disparate). It becomes incumbent upon all who rely on successful communication to understand more fully the factors operating in favor of *and* opposed to communicating.

While certain words signify specific things to librarians, the same may be true for library users, although the signification may vary. Do people coming into a library understand what is meant (implied) by "Reference" or "Circulation?" Rachael Naismith and Joan Stein attempted to test the public's knowledge of some of the terminology commonly used in libraries.[31] They found that there were some terms that a majority of those tested could not identify correctly in a library context. Such terms as "proceedings," "citation," and "clearinghouse" presented problems for the library users. Further examination showed that some correct inferences were made, not by contextual knowledge of the significance of terms, but by the use of linguistic tools or strategies for reasoning. The respondents sometimes placed the term in a more familiar context, based on experience outside the library. Occasionally the respondents examined the structure of the term, breaking the word or phrase down into component parts and making inferences from the subunits. This illustrates what is likely to be a common problem in libraries: What is implied may not be what is inferred, and signification will probably have different foundations for librarians and for users.

It is remarkable that communication is successful as often as it appears to be. Success is an uphill battle; its fight is fraught with the kind of phenomenological caveat offered by Roszak:

> Communication is equivocal. We are limited by a language where words may mean one thing to one person and quite something else to another. There is no ordained right way to communicate. At least in the absolute sense it is impossible to share our thoughts with someone else, for they will not be understood in exactly the same way.[32]

The difficulty is exacerbated if the communication is serial in nature or if there is a single sender and many receivers. In the former instance the implication may change as the role of receiver and sender change. Figure 2.2 is an example of this alteration. With the second case there may be several differing inferences drawn simultaneously as numbers of a group receive the message. Figure 2.3 illustrates this.

One advantage built into the process is that there are multiple "right" ways to communicate. Several of these possibilities might have to be employed in order to succeed, with one receiver or many. The question one may ask in the library environment relates to a primary component of its purpose: Is the increase in information an asset or a liability to the communication process?

Figure 2.2
Receiver Change in Serial Communication

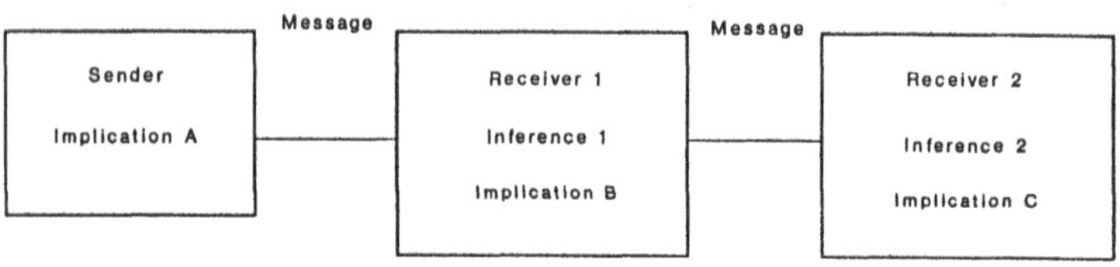

Figure 2.3
Receiver Change in Group Communication

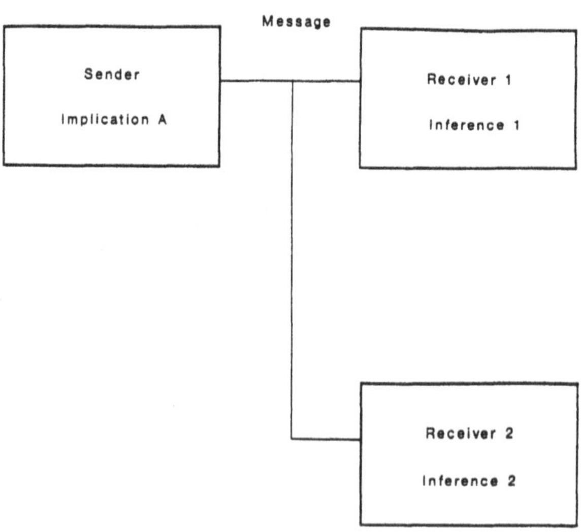

INFORMATION OUTPUT

Growth in Various Media

Meaning formation, obviously, is subject to forces of disruption, to impediments that create possibilities for dysfunction. The statement may sound overly pessimistic and overly cautionary, but much of the business, economics, government, and education on a global scale for the next several decades will be based on exchanges of information. This is not a revelation; it does have a corollary, though. The dependence upon information, for whatever purposes, has led to an increased rate of production of information for the past few decades. The increase has been broad; it has included several media and most disciplines. There are everyday affirmations of the increase: the amount of mail, especially junk mail; the amount of corporate paper (regulations, memoranda, forms); the number of telemarketers; and the number of cable television stations currently available.

In 1983 Ithiel de Sola Pool published the results of an examination of seventeen media from 1960 to 1977.[33] He examined mass media (radio, television, cable television, records and tapes, movies, classroom education, newspapers, magazines, books and direct mail) and point-to-point media (first-class mail, telephone, telex, telegrams, mailgrams, facsimile, and data communication). The number of words made available through the various media grew at a rate of 8.9 percent a year over that time. Further examination revealed that, while the flow of words was greatest in the mass media, the rate of growth was larger in the point-to-point media. With both mass and point-to-point media, growth has been more rapid for electronic forms than for print. The unit cost for production via electronic media fell from 1960 to 1977, while the unit cost for print rose. This growth carries with it implications beyond those of accounting, but the sociological demands and costs will not be addressed here. The works of Marshall McLuhan still provide penetrating insights into the culture of today's society worldwide.

The above trends of general growth of information extend to the scholarly world as well. Derek J. de Solla Price estimated that "depending on what one measures and how, the crude size of science in manpower or in publications tends to double within a period of 10 to 15 years."[34] This particular growth trend is especially evident in the increase of scientific journal articles. Part of the rise in volume of scholarly information in print is attributable to the emphasis on publishing espoused by many universities. In "Measuring Faculty Research Performance," *New Directions in Institutional Research* acknowledged that publication count is perhaps the most common evaluative tool employed by university administrators in assessing faculty.[35] This says nothing of quality, but does provide an objective, easily quantifiable measure. The merits or demerits of such a system of evaluation have been debated and, assuredly, will be debated in the future. Desirability of such a means aside, the practice assures continued growth of scholarly output.

Consumption of Information

More information is produced, but what happens to it? If one hundred cable TV channels are available, a viewer can still watch only one at a time. As choice increases, so, too, will entropy. The same is true for any medium. Pool, in his examination of information flow, found that, while the annual increase in production was 8.9 percent, the growth rate of consumption of words was only 1.2 percent a year from 1960 to 1977.[36] He also observed the constraints on consumption, stating,

> The modesty of that growth in consumption of information, despite the presence of large growth in the information available, is often described as information overload. More and more materials exist, but limitations on time and energy are a controlling barrier to people's consumption of words. Given any particular employment and life-style, there is a limited potential for expansion of attention to media as a whole. Much of that small growth that is found can be accounted for by the shift in population from blue- to white-collar employment and life-styles and the associated rise in educational levels.[37]

The notion of "information overload" has implications, not just for raw consumption of information (the amount of information that can receive marginal attention), but also for more complete processing of the information. Specifically, the flow of information impedes the kind of processing needed to make sense of the individual bits of information, to determine their worth to a particular enterprise—in short, to infer meaning from them. Klapp describes the dilemma of the individual in a state of overload:

> Suppose one is seated at a table fitting pieces of gigantic jigsaw puzzle. From a funnel overhead, pieces are pouring onto the table faster than one can fit them. Most of the pieces do not match—indeed, they do not all belong to the same puzzle. In this metaphor, the pieces of the puzzle represent facts rapidly accumulating; the pattern is the meaning, slowly emerging, perhaps never found.[38]

Klapp also constructs a diagram (Figure 2.4) that illustrates the discrepancy between information, which grows at a substantial rate, and meaning formation, which tends to hold constant.[39] This diagram also serves as a suitable graphic representation of Pool's research findings. At any point in time there is a gap between information and meaning (which is probably the most effective kind of consumption). As time progresses, the gap can only grow larger. As Richard Saul Wurman puts it, "We are like a thirsty person who has been condemned to use a thimble to drink from a fire hydrant."[40] With so much available we tend to think in terms of the degrees of choice and potential, while at the same time facing the realization that a task awaits us that has no end or ultimate resolution. The first part is obvious; there is more being produced than any library can acquire, so the operative choices are felt more dearly than ever before. The second part may not have occurred to all librarians yet; this is not a temporary condition.

Companies and businesses daily hawk products and services supposedly designed to make optimal use of the flood of information. Few of these ads propose to reduce the flow. One tendency is to assume that, as information increases, we "know" more, and our

Figure 2.4
Meaning Lag in Communication

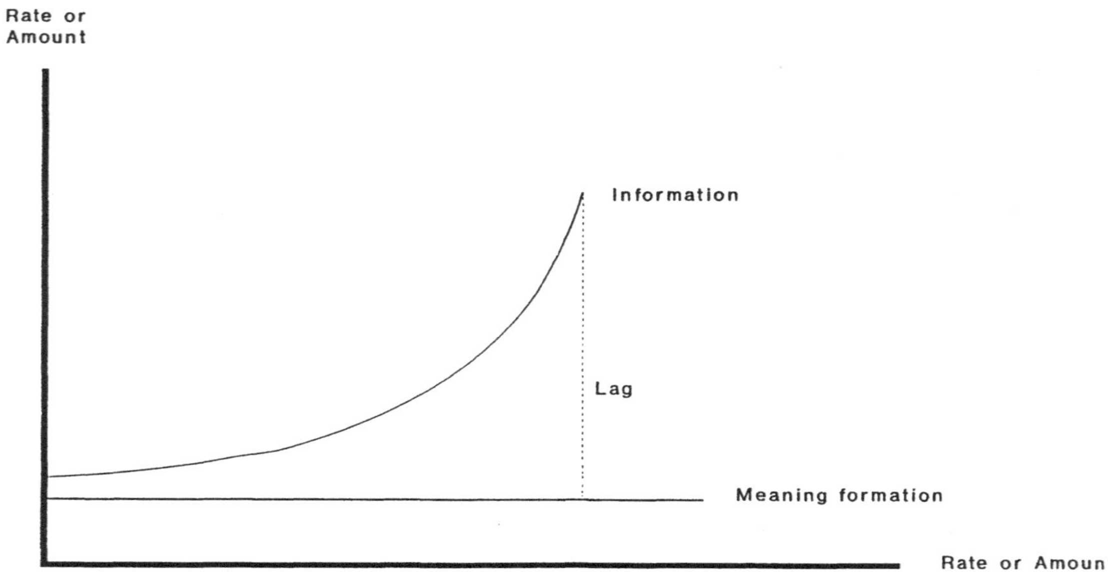

Source: Orrin E. Klapp, "Meaning Lag in an Information Society." *The Journal of Communication* 32 (Spring 82) Copyright 1982. Reprinted with permission of Oxford University Press.

knowledge increases at a rate proportional to the increase in information. Jesse Shera debunks any such claim, recognizing the dynamics of growth and its outcome. He writes,

> Ours is a paper culture, a civilization built on paper bearing symbolic marks. We talk glibly of the "knowledge explosion," but it is not an explosion at all. . . . One could argue that it is our **ignorance**, or at least our awareness of our ignorance, that is "exploding" rather than our knowledge.[41]

One point that Shera makes is that the growth of knowledge is not geometrically regular, but quite irregular, growing quickly in some instances and very slowly in others.

Shera's concept is certainly not widely accepted at this time; at least his articulation of the predicament is at odds with most rhetoric. The more information there is the less intellectual control any individual can have over it. Perhaps the same is true on the institutional level as well. Libraries have uneven difficulties with classification, for instance. New discoveries, new areas of specialized knowledge, create problems for existing classification schemes. These problems are, in part, temporal (there is a time lag between the discovery and the manipulation of the classification schedule to fit it in) and, in part, conceptual (a place must be found for this new specialization). Our access tools, such as the *Library of Congress Subject Headings*, are not equipped to handle the rapid changes in the language of the specializations. In short, as information (rather than knowledge) has exploded, the metainformational structure of the library has had difficulty keeping up.

There are, of course, prices to be paid for the "meaning lag," for the gap between the flow of information and its consumption. The price is entropy. Klapp indicates:

> What such negative elements in the appetite for information suggest is that along with the growth of information there has been a decline in its marginal value of meaning. The point might be made with the economist's idea of marginal utility. Yet another useful economic analogy is that the

decline of value of information was rather like an inflation of currency: the more there was of it, the less it seemed to "buy" in meaning.[42]

The cost can be seen in real terms. For instance, in 1964 a paper was published in the journal *Lancet* linking the intake of sucrose with heart disease. Perhaps because of overload, among some other factors, the paper was not attended to and much of the research leading to its publication was repeated by others ten years later.[43] Simply because there is more does not mean that "good" information is preserved at the expense of "bad." This phenomenon is complicated because "good" and "bad" are, in many instances, relative and cannot be determined absolutely.

Growth of Information Available in Libraries

The information overload may be nowhere more evident than in libraries, which exist to collect, organize, and retrieve information. Libraries are being greeted by the overload on numerous fronts, including both traditional and less traditional technologies. Statistical trends contradict predictions of the demise of the book. For instance, in 1977 the title output for the United States, including hardbound and paperbound titles, was 42,780.[44] This may seem a daunting figure, but the output for 1987 was 56,027, an increase of nearly 31 percent.[45] The United States was not alone in realizing a substantial increase. The total output of titles in Britain in 1978 was 38,766; by 1988 the number rose to 62,063, an increase of about 60 percent.[46]

The output figures point to challenges (a euphemism for problems) for virtually all libraries. A research library with formidable resources will be hard-pressed just to keep up with U.S. and British production. Publications from other nations, plus desiderata lists, ensure that very few libraries can keep up with needed acquisitions. Smaller libraries find themselves in entropic predicaments; the degree of choice is likely to be quite high. Librarians question whether they are making the most cost-beneficial purchases. Even in the face of these limitations libraries acquire large numbers of materials. In fiscal year 1988 alone, university libraries that are members of the Association of Research Libraries (ARL) added a gross total of 8,362,893 volumes to their collections.[47] In that same year, one hundred Association of College and Research Libraries (ACRL) university libraries added 2,313,240.[48]

One direct effect of the increase in the library holdings of books is a swelling of the library's catalog. New entries must be added to the catalog, whether its format is cards or machine-readable records. With each new entry, additional access points are added, creating additional choices for the library user. The question of whether this is a boon or a bane to the user will be addressed in Chapter 4.

In addition to the increase in book production, the journal literature has grown over the last several years. Indexing and abstracting tools have ballooned to cover the increase in this form of communication. Not only have many reference sources increased the numbers of journals covered, but the numbers of articles indexed have propagated, sometimes at a disproportionately high rate. Table 2.1 illustrates the rapid growth of the literature, as evidenced in selected sources.

A similar pattern is apparent in *Science Citation Index* (SCI). From 1977 to 1987 the number of source journal items (articles indexed) increased from 494,861 to 621,308. The total number of citations analyzed in these source items grew from 7,271,526 in 1977 to 10,100,820 in 1987. Not only did the gross number of citations grow, but the number of citations to unique items increased from 3,776,247 to 4,907,383. More than a million items made their way into the scientific literature via the citation route during this period. Citations received by individual journal titles have also grown during recent years. Citations made in a given year to a journal's issues published in the preceding two years are tracked by SCI. For instance, indexers count the references in articles published in all covered journals this year to a particular journal's articles published in the issues of last year and the year before. These individual journals referred to by this year's articles are then ranked by frequency of citation. Table 2.2 shows how citations have increased from 1980 to 1987.[49]

Table 2.1
Growth of Articles Indexed in Selected Publications

Title	Number of Articles in 1978	Number of Articles in 1988	Percentage Growth
Biological Abstracts	74,502	131,030	75.9
Chemical Abstracts	225,717	243,077	7.7
Computers and Control Abstracts	32,047	66,209	106.6
Engineering Index	95,384	120,337	26.2
Mathematical Reviews	32,646	94,050	188.1
Physical Abstracts (Science Abstracts, Series A)	96,582	143,030	48.1
Psychological Abstracts	26,293	37,637	43.1

Table 2.2
Growth in Citations Received by Top-Ranked Journals

Journal Rank	Citations in 1980 to 1978 and 1979	Citations in 1987 to 1985 and 1986	Percentage Growth
1	24,398	36,493	49.6
10	10,125	14,411	42.3
25	5,366	7,425	38.4
50	3,692	4,685	26.9
100	1,799	2,294	27.5

The growth has been likewise impressive in nontraditional areas. In the early 1970s an innovation known as online searching arrived on the information and library scenes. This represented something of a change in kind as well as a change in quantity of available information. Now there are thousands of available databases from hundreds of producers. Major vendors of databases, such as Dialog and BRS, constantly increase the number of databases available through them and libraries are expected to translate this availability into service to their communities. The result is not only an increase in information, but also an increase in the complexity of access to the information. In the 1980s the growth medium has been CD-ROM technology, which has produced further pressure on libraries as information suppliers. These new products and services, aimed primarily at access, create a situation of potential overload for library users before the users even get to the information itself.

Are the increased library holdings and services consumed by libraries' users? Is meaning increasing as the number of books, journals, and other forms of information do? Are the dysfunctions that plague communication in society at large common to communication in libraries? Let me attempt to answer these questions with an example of literature in an emerging scientific field. One area of research in physics that has developed over the last twenty years has focused on constructing a Grand Unified Theory, or a Theory of Everything. One branch of this work put forth mathematical models in which matter is composed of strings. Initial efforts concentrated on a connection between this different structure of matter and subatomic particles called hadrons. When interest in the connections between the two waned, only a handful of scientists kept working on string theory, and their work received little attention. The lack of interest during the 1970s was reflected in the literature and its tools of access. Key papers received few citations and *Science Citation Index*'s "Permuterm Subject Index" contained no references before 1980 to superstring or superstrings (which the theory became known as) and very few to string theory.

Interest in the theory was reignited in the 1980s, and the growth reflected in the literature has been dramatic. From 1980 through 1984 only 12 entries were available under superstring(s) in the permuterm index. In 1985 alone the number increased to 58, and in 1986 to 156. By 1987 there were a total of 289 entries listed for string theory and superstring(s). The literature depicts extremes of the communication problem in libraries. During the early years of work in this area papers written on the subject were largely inaccessible, at least from certain points. In a matter of just a few years the dilemma of paucity became one of plethora, and overload set in. The increase in publishing activity caused access to specific items to deteriorate because so many entries were indexed under a few basic terms. Working scientists, who use other means to communicate, are usually not affected by such a phenomenon, but in an emerging field scientists and students might be entering from other, related areas and might not be plugged into the informal networks that are likely to be in place. The importance of the formal literature and the library are thus enlarged. The increase in the bulk of the literature may diminish its effectiveness.

The above example illustrates the potential diseconomy of scale, which is not limited to academic libraries or reserach materials. Charles Robinson upbraids public libraries for seeing themselves as repositories, which he views as an expensive and ineffective proposition.[50] Overload can occur at any level with any user group. The environment external to libraries is not likely to change soon, so libraries must balance optimization of meaning with burgeoning production. This will be the fruit of further discussion, but first let us look at the structure of the communication process.

NOTES

1. P. Dorn, "The Nature of Information" *Business Information Systems*, InfoTech State of the Art Report, series 9, no. 7, Pergamon-Infotech, 1981, quoted in R. K. Stamper, "Towards a Theory of Information: Information: Mystical Fluid or a Subject for Scientific Inquiry?" *Computer Journal*, 28, no. 3 (1985), 195.

2. F. Keay, *The Numerate Manager* (London: Allen and Unwin, 1969), quoted in Stamper, "Towards a Theory of Information," 195.

3. R. K. Stamper, "Towards a Theory of Information: Information: Mystical Fluid or a Subject for Scientific Inquiry?" *Computer Journal*, 28, no. 3 (1985), 195–99.

4. Pauline Wilson, "Mission or Information: What Business Are We In?" *Journal of Academic Librarianship*, 14 (May 1988), 84.

5. Fritz Machlup, "Semantic Quirks in Studies of Information," in *The Study of Information*, ed. Fritz Machlup and Una Mansfield (New York: Wiley, 1983), 642–44.

6. Donald M. MacKay, *Information, Mechanism, and Meaning* (Cambridge: Massachusetts Institute of Technology Press, 1969), 11.

7. Christopher John Fox, *Information and Misinformation: An Investigation of the Notions of Information, Misinformation, Informing, and Misinforming* (Westport, CT: Greenwood Press, 1983).

8. Fred I. Dretske, *Knowledge and the Flow of Information* (Cambridge: Massachusetts Institute of Technology, 1981), 45.

9. Wilson, "Mission or Information," 84–85.

10. Theodore Roszak, *The Cult of Information* (New York: Pantheon, 1986).

11. Harlan Cleveland, "Information as a Resource," *Futurist*, 16 (December 1982), 35–36.

12. Thomas S. Kuhn, *The Structure of Scientific Revolutions*, 2nd. ed. (Chicago: University of Chicago Press, 1970).

13. Umberto Eco, *A Theory of Semiotics* (Bloomington: Indiana University Press, 1976), 8–9.

14. Walker Percy, *The Message in the Bottle* (New York: Farrar, Straus and Giroux, 1975), 246.

15. Charles S. Peirce, *Collected Papers* (Cambridge, MA: Harvard University Press, 1931–1958), cited in Percy, *The Message in the Bottle*, 251.

16. Percy, *The Message in the Bottle*, pp. 251–52.

17. Umberto Eco, *Semiotics and the Philosophy of Language* (Bloomington: Indiana University Press, 1984), 15.

18. Warren Weaver, "The Mathematics of Communication," *Scientific American*, 181 (July 1949), 11.

19. Colin Cherry, *On Human Communication: A Review, a Survey, and a Criticism*, 3rd ed. (Cambridge: Massachusetts Institute of Technology Press, 1978), 74.

20. David K. Berlo, *The Process of Communication* (New York: Holt, Rinehart, and Winston, 1960), 2.

21. Ibid., 175.

22. C. K. Ogden and I. A. Richards, *The Meaning of Meaning: A Study of the Influence of Language Upon Thought and of the Science of Symbolism* (San Diego: Harvest/Harcourt Brace Jovanovich, 1989), 1–23.

23. Berlo, *The Process of Communication*, 43.
24. Paul Watzlawick, Janet Helmick Beavin, and Don D. Jackson, *Pragmatics of Human Communication: A Study of Interactional Patterns, Pathologies, and Paradoxes* (New York: W. W. Norton & Co., 1967), 21.
25. Willis Jackson, ed., *Communication Theory* (New York: Academic Press, 1953), 2.
26. Niklas Luhmann, "The Improbability of Communication," *International Social Science Journal*, 33 (1981), 123.
27. Orrin E. Klapp, "Meaning Lag in an Information Society," *Journal of Communication*, 32 (Spring 1982), 56.
28. Ibid., 58.
29. Weaver, "The Mathematics of Communication," 15.
30. Paul Kecskemeti, *Meaning, Communication, and Value* (Chicago: University of Chicago Press, 1952), 5–6.
31. Rachael Naismith and Joan Stein, "Library Jargon: Student Comprehension of Technical Language Used by Librarians," *College & Research Libraries*, 50 (September 1989), 543–52.
32. Rozsak, *The Cult of Information*, 102.
33. Ithiel de Sola Pool, "Tracking the Flow of Information," *Science*, 221 (12 August 1983), 609–13.
34. Derek J. de Solla Price, *Little Science, Big Science . . . and Beyond* (New York: Columbia University Press, 1986), 5.
35. John W. Creswell, ed., "Measuring Faculty Research Performance," *New Directions for Institutional Research*, no. 50 (June 1986).
36. Pool, "Tracking the Flow of Information," 609.
37. Ibid.
38. Klapp, "Meaning Lag in an Information Society," 58.
39. Ibid., 60.
40. Richard Saul Wurman, *Information Anxiety* (New York: Doubleday, 1989), 36.
41. Jesse H. Shera, *Introduction to Library Science: Basic Elements of Library Service* (Littleton, CO: Libraries Unlimited, 1976), 58–59.
42. Orrin E. Klapp, *Overload and Boredom: Essays on the Quality of Life in the Information Society* (Westport, CT: Greenwood Press, 1986), 9.
43. Charles L. Bernier and A. Neil Yerkey, *Cogent Communication: Overcoming Reading Overload* (Westport, CT: Greenwood Press, 1979), 3–6.
44. *Bowker Annual of Library and Book Trade Information* (New York: R. R. Bowker, 1979), 322.
45. *Bowker Annual of Library and Book Trade Information* (New York: R. R. Bowker, 1989), 425.
46. Ibid., 444.

47. Association of Research Libraries, *ARL Statistics, 1987–1988* (Washington, DC: Association of Research Libraries, 1989), 29.

48. Robert E. Molyneux, comp., *ACRL University Library Statistics, 1987–1988* (Chicago: Association of College and Research Libraries, 1989), 25.

49. Institute for Scientific Information, *Science Citation Index, Journal Citation Reports, 1980* (Philadelphia: ISI, 1981), 175, and *Science Citation Index, Journal Citation Reports 1987* (Philadelphia: ISI, 1988), 203.

50. Charles Robinson, "Can We Save the Public's Library?" *Library Journal*, 114 (September 1989), 147–52.

3

What Does a Communication Process Look Like?

QUESTIONS FOR COMMUNICATIONS RESEARCH

The intent of Chapter 1 was to provide a cursory introduction to some of the ways that various individuals and schools of thought look at libraries, information, and communication. Chapter 2 focused on information and sought to answer questions regarding the place of information in a library, the relationship of information and meaning, and how (and how fast) information grows. This chapter focuses more directly on communication; it tries to come to grips with communication's fluidity and tenuousness. This, of course, necessitates a perception of communication as a process—a continuous, multidirectional flow—engaged in by varying numbers of participants. As a process, communication is not easy to study; it refuses to stand still long enough for scrutiny. The problems associated with the examination of communication are somewhat similar to those faced by physicists.

One of the things a researcher usually attempts when examining any process is to break that process down to its component parts—preferably to the smallest parts measurable. This is certainly problematic with communication. How small can parts get? It may be possible, at least with some kinds of communication, to get down to the level of bits of information. (Bits is used here more in the way that computer or systems scientists might use the term, not as a measure of uncertainty, as Claude Shannon defined it.) For some aspects of study, such as levels of redundancy in language, this may be quite fruitful. For other aspects, such as behavioral effects of communication, this strategy could be overly reductionist. One could imagine a debate in communication circles somewhat akin to that which arose several decades ago in physics. Is communication comprised of waves or particles? As was true of physics, there is likely to be an uncertainty principle, whereby some kinds of observation are suited to the study of certain properties of communication, but not to others. I do not mean to imply that a scientific approach should govern research in this area, only that some of the questions that have been asked in the sciences may be reasonably asked in communication and information studies.

Another approach that has arisen in the sciences that may have some import for communication is chaos theory. There is a substantial amount of randomness in communication, especially considering the fluidity of the process and the changing roles of individuals in it. Just as weather patterns are influenced by a complex set of variable forces, so, too, is communication. In fact, the probability of a particular individual receiving and understanding a given message may be as difficult, if not more difficult, to predict as tomorrow's weather. One of the difficulties with prediction of receipt and understanding is common to dynamical systems—determining the initial state of the system. Exactly where does a message originate? If that could be answered, what forces act on the process? These include language of sender and receiver, channel selection, size of audience, noise, and myriad other forces. Despite the difficulty of achieving precision, the researcher needs to be aware of the complexity of the process and, perhaps, to be sensitized to the possibilities that chaos implies.

LINEAR COMMUNICATION MODELS

Researchers have, in the past, sought an explanation for, or at least a description of, the communication process. Most of these models take the form Ronald Smith refers to as verbal-pictorial.[1] There is usually a graphic representation of the process, accompanied by some indication of direction of flow. It may be tempting to foist a tautology on readers by way of explaining the purpose of models and say that models represent things. This they do, but the definition offered by Karl Deutsch is more descriptive and more useful: a model presents a set of symbols and operating rules that are intended to match corresponding relevant points in some existing structure or process.[2] Its purpose is to present a means of organizing data or elements into a coherent structure, to allow for the measurement of phenomena, to permit the prediction of future states, or to reveal hitherto unknown facts or relationships.

Modeling the communication process is not a simple task. For reasons noted above, many factors influence the process; identifying the factors, even the major ones, and placing them in the context of the possible relationships can be difficult. Because of this most models purposely aim for simplification and provide something of a coarse snapshot of the process—a picture of what might be occurring at a given point in time. Some models focus on dyadic human communication; that is, exchanges between two people. Certain assumptions are frequently made in the interest of simplification: the individuals share a common language, attention can be focused by the individuals on the exchange, and noise is minimal. As has been discussed in the previous chapter, the first assumption is not necessarily a safe one and, even when a basic language is shared, there may be sufficient local or regional variances to obfuscate the process. Allowance for all possible variances, though, would quickly negate the utility of the model.

Because of the complexity of communication any model must be flexible enough to allow the vagaries of components or elements. Klaus Krippendorff prescribes some criteria that a usable model should consider:

- Information about the identity of the basic communicators of the source and their respective boundaries.
- Information about the states of each component of the source, including the communicators' possible perceptions of the situation, their communication and behavioral strategies, evaluative frameworks, and objectives.
- Information about the transmission facilities, time delays, channels, and stable relations between the communicators.
- Information about the existing constraints that have evolved in the course of previous interactions; that is, the system's basic operating rules and parameters, the definition of the situation and of the communicators' roles, shared or not.
- Information about the mechanism of control and the regulating power of the exchanged verbalization that structures those mechanisms.
- Information about the hierarchical structure and quantity of knowledge available to the communicators about the possible dynamic interdependence between the source's components.[3]

One early verbal model of communication was offered by Harold Lasswell: "Who Says What In Which Channel To Whom With What Effect?"[4] The elements Lasswell identified have been incorporated into many subsequent models. One aspect of this articulation—and a possible drawback of it—is that it is unidirectional. It travels only one way and, so, is controlled by the emenator of the message. As Werner Severin and James Tankard point out, "Lasswell's model has been criticized because it seems to imply the presence of a communicator and a purposive message."[5] There is no doubt that there is a communicator; the "who" in the statement is originating the process and, implicitly, is making decisions regarding content and medium. The model could be applied to dyadic communication and to much mass communication. However, to read that the message is necessarily purposive is to limit the model. Another implication of the model is that the message is received ("to whom"). Receipt of the message is, almost invariably, going to have some effect, even if there is no purposive effect intended. A simple declarative statement is likely to have some effect on the receiver. That effect need not be, and in most instances will not be, profound.

One thing that can be said about Lasswell's model is that it is linear. It has a point of origination; it travels a certain path; it has a stopping point. Of course the process does not end there, but the identities of the "who" and "to whom" are certainly subject to change. The elements of Lasswell's statement became graphic and verbal representations in the model devised in 1949 by Shannon and Weaver (see Figure 3.1).[6]

The intent behind the work of Shannon was to investigate the nature of technical communication, with an eye, eventually, to improving its fidelity. This model is influenced by certain properties of information and communication discussed in Chapter 1, such as degree of choice (entropy) and redundancy. One of the efforts behind technical communication is the reduction of noise, which leads to greater efficiency of the process. As Lasswell's statement, the model of Shannon and Weaver is linear—a message has a source and it travels in a certain direction to a destination. While this may seem to be a limitation, it is important to keep in mind that its accuracy is dependent on the technical features of some

Figure 3.1
Shannon/Weaver Model

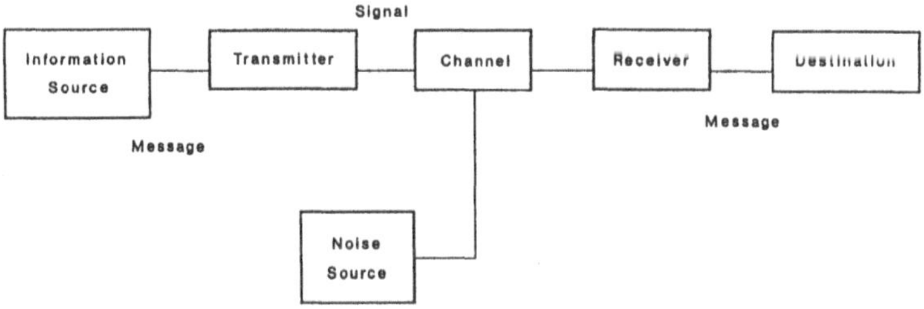

Source: Claude E. Shannon and Warren Weaver, *The Mathematical Theory of Communication* (Urbana: University of Illinois Press, 1949), pp. 7, 34. Copyright 1949, The University of Illinois Press. Reprinted with permission of the publisher.

kinds of communication. For instance, messages on telephone lines are unidirectional and do have identifiable sources and destinations.

While the Shannon and Weaver scheme is intended to be representative of technical communication, it has been reproduced frequently as an adequate description of human communication. Some, however, such as C. E. Osgood, eschew this kind of use of the model. Osgood's own work centered on the psycholinguistic process and attempted to account for meaning as well as the sending and receipt of messages. He recognized the immutable multiplicity of roles that humans have in the communication process; they function as both sources and destinations. At various times, and occasionally simultaneously, a person is engaged in encoding and decoding and shifting of roles is very fluid. In human communication, according to Osgood, the process has a distinct motor function; the sender provides a stimulus that generates a response on the part of the receiver. Each individual contains both the functions of source and those of destinations; the characteristics of transmitter and those of receiver.[7]

The communication act involves more than one unit. In such an act a stimulus generally elicits a response that, in turn, can act as a stimulus. The stimuli are not limited to linguistic utterances; they can be far-ranging and varied. Osgood describes the social nature of the act:

> When individual A talks to individual B, for example, his postures, gestures, facial expressions and even manipulations with objects (e.g., laying down a playing card, pushing a bowl of food within reach) may all be a part of the message, as of course are events in the sound wave channel. But other parts of A's total behavior (e.g., sensations from B's own posture, cues from the remainder of the environment) do not derive from A's behavior—these events are not part of the message as we use the term. These R-S message events (reactions of one individual that produce stimuli for another) may be either immediate or mediate—ordinary face-to-face conversation illustrates the former and written communication (along with musical recordings, art objects, and so forth) illustrates the latter.[8]

His graphic representation illustrates the several layers at which the process can be observed.[9] The levels of Osgood's model include the motor-related functions inherent in phonetics, which involves articulation on the part of the sender, and psychoacoustics, which is central to the act of hearing on the part of the receiver. Also included are the complex mental processes of message formulation and interpretation and communication as a social act between or among individuals.

Other researchers have stood on the shoulders of both Shannon and Osgood. This, of course, necessitates a union of the technical model with the linguistically-related one. One of these researchers, Wilbur Schramm, constructed variant models that attempted to build on features of both. Schramm altered Shannon's basic linear model to include what can be seen as at once the psycholinguistic and the social facets of Osgood's scheme (see Figure 3.2).[10] Each participant in the process—the sender and the receiver—has an individual field of experience. Experience encompasses language, learning, environment, and other personal and social variables. Communication occurs in the context of the experience that is shared by the participants. Schramm notes,

Figure 3.2
Schramm Model

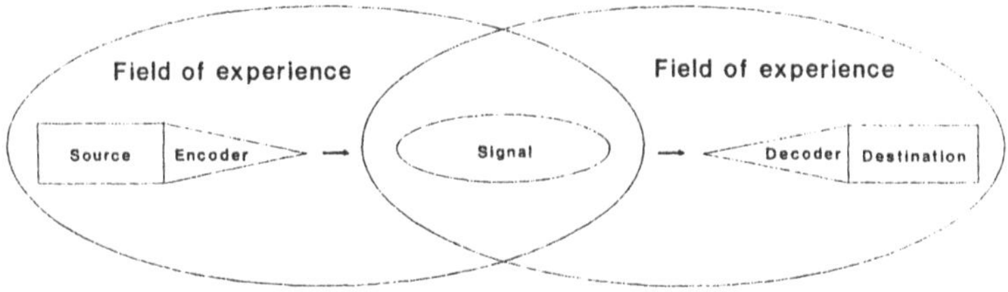

Source: Wilbur Schramm, "How Communication Works," *The Process and Effects of Mass Communication* (Urbana: University of Illinois, 1954): 22. Copyright 1954, The University of Illinois Press. Reprinted with permission of the publisher.

> If the circles have a large area in common, then communication is easy. If the circles do not meet—if there has been no common experience—then communication is impossible. If the circles have only a small area in common—that is, if the experiences of source and destination have been strikingly unlike—then it is going to be very difficult to get an intended meaning across from one to the other.[11]

For instance, if a teacher says, "Andrew Marvell's 'To His Coy Mistress' is an excellent illustration of *carpe diem*," to a student who knows not a word of Latin, a portion of the message will not be decoded by the student. The fields of experience do not overlap sufficiently for complete understanding to occur. This model, while elaborating on the abilities and limitations of the human participants, is still linear. Schramm's model does allow for feedback, but in this iteration feedback signifies primarily the reversal of roles between source and destination.

Field of experience implies interpretation—something not common to many of the models noted thusfar. As can be seen from the models, once the message reaches the receiver, the process is complete. In practical terms it is far from complete. The decoding event is not based solely on arriving at definitions of words comprising the message, although that is the first stage. Beyond that comes the cognitive process of interpreting the message, seeking something relevant in it that can be applied to the receiver's physical, emotional, or intellectual makeup. Further, the same message sent to different receivers may result in differing interpretations. What is likely to happen is that each receiver has choices among varying possible interpretations, one of which is the intended interpretation. The other interpretations may result in inferences of meaning that are at odds with implied meaning. Figure 3.3 points out a simplified schema of possibilities when a message is sent to multiple receivers. In the case of Figure 3.3, Interpretation 1 would have been the appropriate event for Receiver A. However, for some reason (decoding dysfunction, noise, etc.), a blockage prevented inference of meaning to match implication of meaning. This extension of the linear models allows for potentially improved understanding of the workings of communication.

Figure 3.3
Interpretive Possibilities with Multiple Receivers

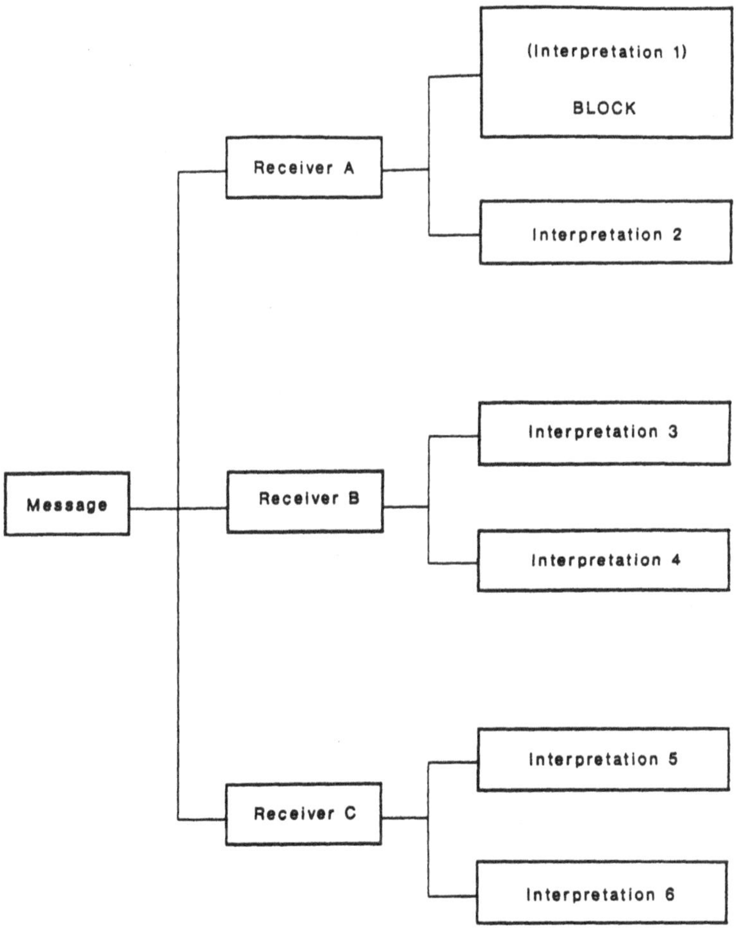

Nonlinear Communication Models

Human communication is even more complex than technical communication. The models discussed so far are limited in that they assume that, at any given time, one person (system) is acting as source (who is encoding and transmitting) and another as destination (who is receiving and decoding). Frank Dance writes, "The linear model betrays reality in not providing for a modification of communicative behavior in the future based upon communicative success or shortcomings in the past."[12] One way to envision the difference between the linear models discussed and what Dance is speaking of is to consider that one way humans learn is heuristically. A person remembers what worked and didn't work in the past and adjusts future behavior accordingly. The geometric figure Dance chooses to represent communication is the helix. He writes, "The communication process, like the helix, is constantly moving forward and yet is always to some degree dependent upon the past, which informs the present and the future."[13]

The helical model of Dance, however, focuses on only one person and that person's experiences brought to and taken from a communication exchange. While it is illustrative of an ergodic process (that is, a stochastic process that is statistically regular), it cannot cope with the duality, or even multiplicity, of roles or states that any one individual occupies in the course of an exchange. As Thomas Sebeok observes, "The individual human functions more or less simultaneously as both [source and destination]—indeed, he regularly decodes through various homeostatic mechanisms the messages he himself has encoded."[14] Sebeok's model is hexagonal, building upon the triadic one of Buhler (see Figure 3.4).[15]

> It would seem useful not to expand this triadic model into a hexagonal one, which involves the following dimensions: (I) an Addressor (or actor) who selects—i.e., encodes according to specific statistical constraints—(V) a message out of (VI) a code which must be—to permit decoding—fully or at least partially shared by (II) and addressee (or reactor); the message also requires (III) a referent (or, better, context) and (IV) a "channel" allowing the participants to establish and maintain contact.

Figure 3.4
Sebeok Model

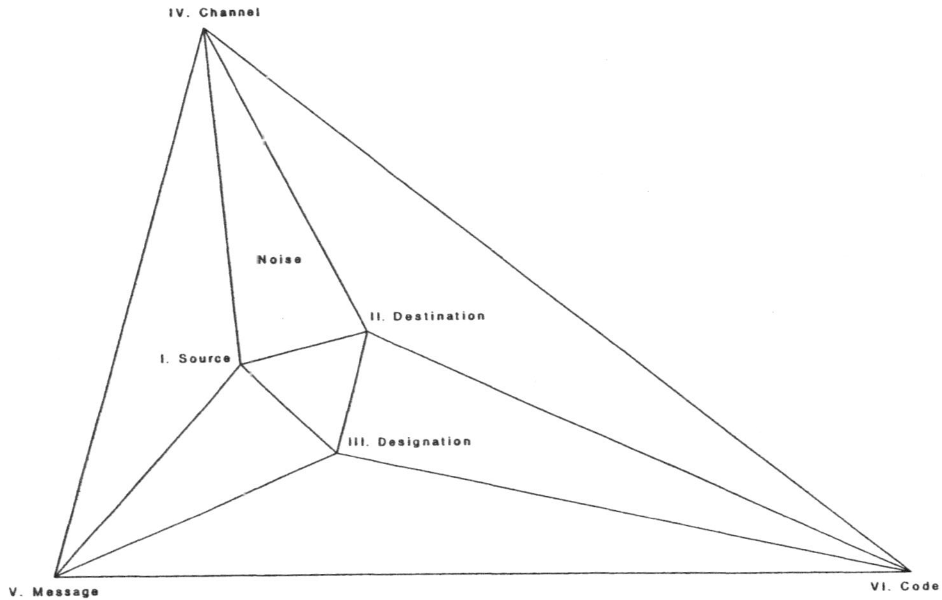

Source: "Coding in the Evolution of Signalling Behavior," By Thomas A. Sebeok, *Behavioral Science*, vol. 7 (October 1962): 433. Reprinted with permission of the journal.

(That portion of a communication which intrudes into the message en route from source to receiver is noise; it is mixed intimately, although in varying proportions, with the signal—that portion of a communication which originates with the addresser.)[16]

Sebeok's model makes clearer the importance of shared language, but it does not deal as extensively with social aspects as does Schramm's.

Sebeok's model has been built upon by Robert A. Fairthorne. As does Sebeok's, Fairthorne's model consists of six elements: channel, codes, and messages (incorporated from Shannon); and sources, destinations, and designations. The first three elements form the core of the signaling function, which can be examined, in part, in isolation from other aspects of the communication process. Such a study does not concern itself with the nature of the source or of what is communicated. The last three elements are separate from the signaling apparatus. Fairthorne explains these features thusly:

> When considered by itself the triad, Source, Destination, Designation, constitutes Discourse as such. That is, it suffices for study of those aspects of communication that are independent of particular modes of representation on the one hand, and particular characteristics (including existence) of what is talked about on the other. Thus it forms the ceiling of our black box, because we cannot go beyond it without taking part in the discourse ourselves.
>
> To do this is to change our scope and function completely, just as to change from typist to author is to change one's scope and function completely, even if one continues to type.[17]

He combines these two sets of elements in a hexagonal model that is very similar to Sebeok's. The various activities of the communication process can be reduced to any of several triads—combinations of three elements connected to one another as illustrated in the model. The activities include reception, authorship, and transmission. The ways the elements are combined depict the nature of the particular activity. For instance, as Fairthorne notes, the activity may involve coding the use of a given Message set to suit the characteristics of a physical Channel. This is an aspect of Signaling. . . . Coding the use of a given Message set to suit its Designation is not an aspect of Signaling, but of Subject Classification, that is, establishment of a code to link a set of messages with a set of topics, subject matter, or user interests.[18]

Fairthorne focuses, in his paper, on a small group of combinations that transcend the mechanical process of signaling. His analysis seems at once complex and elegant. It isn't that he doesn't recognize a greater range of possibilities; rather, he chooses to direct his attention on a set of activities central to the flow of information. Of the seven activities he focuses on (see model), only one, signaling, does not involve either source or destination. In fact, his concept of flow dictates that action by source or destination is essential. That there must be at least potential for Signaling—the physical transmission of a message, including a shared code—is taken for granted if there is to be a flow of information (see Figure 3.5).

Examination of Fairthorne's model suggests that there are more combinations than he describes. Calvin Mooers examines the remaining possibilities. The model, broken down into its component parts, is composed of twenty triads. Mooers attempts to name those not classified by Fairthorne. For instance, the Codes–Designations–Sources triad is one passed over by Fairthorne, but Mooers observes that one interpretation of this set is a means of placing authors (Sources) into categoriess based on the subjects of their works (Designations) using a naming or classification system (Code) for categorization.[19] This he names "A Classification System upon or of Authors."

Mooers also recognizes that there is no set description for each of the six elements of the model. The mathematical equivalent of differing forms of each element is the partial derivative that, while a linear measure, is equipped to deal with variables comprised of a set of attributes. The attributes may change in differing situations or when acted upon by various forces. In addition to this partial derivative concept, Mooers admits that varying levels of entropy

Figure 3.5
Fairthorne Model II

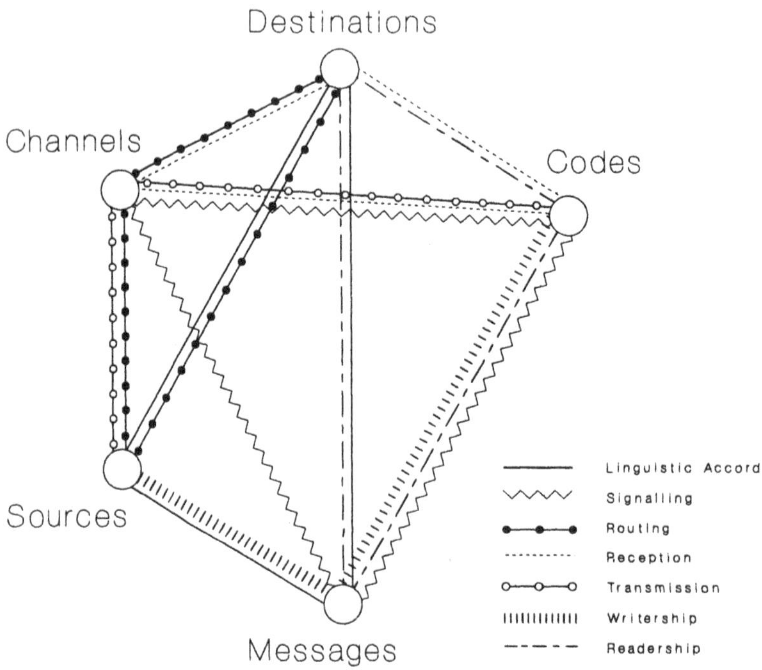

Source: Robert A. Fairthorne, "Morphology of 'Information Flow'," *Journal of the Association for Computing Machinery*, 14 (October 1967), 717. Copyright 1967, Association for Computing Machinery, Inc. Reprinted with permission of the ACM.

also affect the activities and the natures of the elements. If differences in classification or in levels of entropy are subtle, the number of permutations the twenty triads may be subject to is very high indeed. Fairthorne and Mooers provide a limited description of the major classes of activities within the communication process and information flow. That the description is limited is necessary. We first need an explanation of the basic elements, which they help us understand, before we can attempt to grasp the many variations the elements may take.

These later models differ from that of Shannon in ways that go beyond differences in or levels of simplicity and elaborateness. Most of these are built on a different premise, which Dean Barnlund states explicitly: "The distinction being suggested here is between systems that are deterministic and mechanical, and those that are spontaneous and discretionary."[20] Human communication is based on the latter and, so, will behave in ways different from technical or mechanical systems. Predictability in a technical system is possible in the sense that output can be surmised if input is known. The logic governing the system is not particularly flexible and is frequently based on a series of binary decisions, so an understanding of the system includes an understanding of the path it will take given a certain set of data. Human behavior exhibits other properties that are not absolutely unrepeatable (which would produce an entropy level of 1) but that can be unpredictable. Barnlund states,

> People do display consistency in behavior, the degree of consistency reflecting the rigidity of assumptions required by the personality to maintain itself in encounters with reality. But, while behavior patterns may reappear from time to time, normally they do not repeat themselves precisely, nor are they triggered by identical environmental cues.[21]

Barnlund attempts to account for some of the contingencies affecting the communication process in his model. The import of both public and private cues is evident here. If two people are in conversation, each may be aware of the surroundings, such as the home or office of one of the persons (public cue). Each may also be aware of private cues, such as memories of experiences or readings from the past that may influence the current situation. Messages are then transmitted through both verbal and nonverbal means. It is possible that the two means may even be contradictory in some circumstances. Finally, the encoding and decoding processes are not separate and discreet, but are interrelated. One is dependent on the other, and one may change as the other is altered. These facets of Barnlund's model illustrate the difficulty of prediction by pointing out some of the classes of interdictory and enabling forces likely to be at work at any given time.

Other writers incorporate, sometimes implicitly, some of the points Barnlund made in constructing and describing his model. David Campbell and Dale Level, for instance, pay special attention to the emergence of meaning through communication. Their model is presented in Figure 3.6.[22] Symbolic interpretation is an important element of the model and occurs at various stages of the process. The focus of Campbell and Level is purposive communication—that which is intended to produce a desired behavior or outcome. Because of the directedness of this kind of communication, the sender in this configuration encodes a message on the basis of perceptions of the receiver's symbolic interpretation apparatus. That is, the sender will refer to previous observations or other first-hand and second-hand knowledge of the receiver and will construct a message based on probability of the receiver interpreting the message in the way it was intended. Campbell and Level do note that "Meanings cannot be imposed on any person by any other person. Each person makes his own interpretation of all stimuli, even if the interpretation is not conscious."[23]

From the standpoint of the receiver there are potential roadblocks to the emergence of meaning as intended by the sender. Although Campbell and Level are writing from the perspective of communication in the business world, the basis of their model and its applicability to analysis of the dynamics of interchange has broader relevance. One element they separate from symbolic interpretation is the receiver's value system. The separation is a recognition of both the objective components of interpretation and the subjective, which may be less rational and more volatile. The model also accounts for external factors, which may either support or conflict with the message sent. With some forms of communication, such as direct written communication or even telephone communication, the sender may be unaware of certain environmental interference. This potential obstruction is evident in the model when the sender attempts to interpret the behavior of the receiver. Campbell and Level consolidate the possible imbroglio

Figure 3.6
Campbell/Level Model

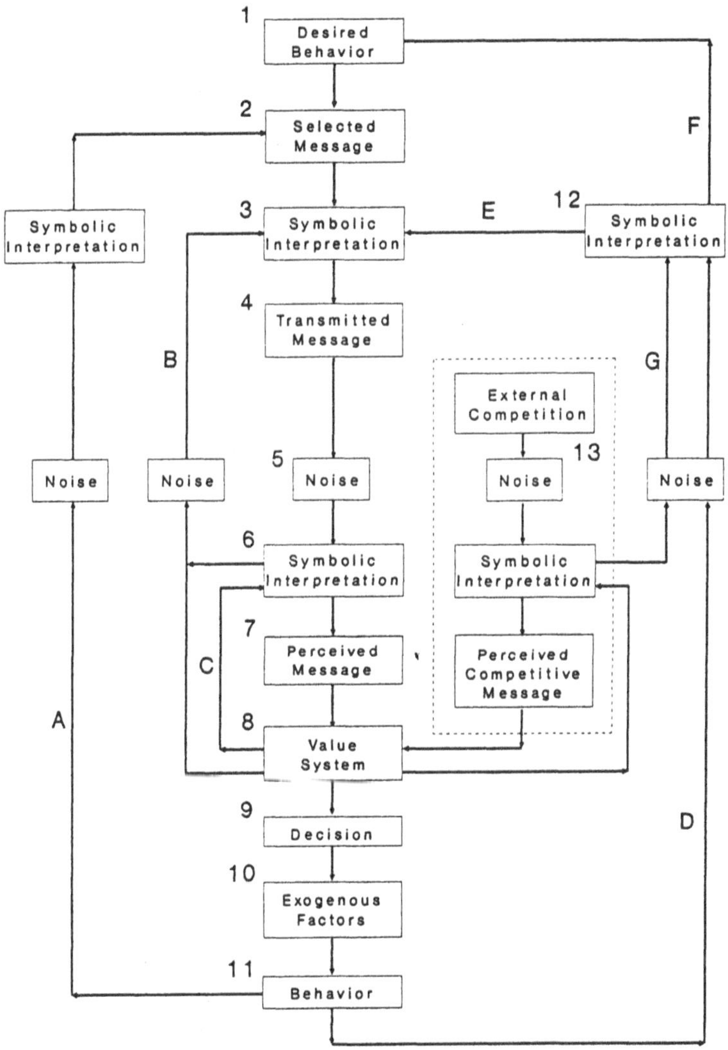

Source: David P. Campbell and Dale Level, "A Black Box Model of Communication," *Journal of Business Communication* 22 (Summer 1985): 40. Reprinted with permission of David P. Campbell.

by noting that "at best, the sender possesses only limited knowledge of the receiver's interpretive system, the effects of competitive messages, the effects of the various interactions present in the system, and the effects of noise on all pathways."[24]

Some of the commonality necessary for meaning to be formed is identified by Campbell and Level; Andrew Targowski and Joel Bowman take the notion of a contextual net yet further with their model, shown in Figure 3.7.[25] This model is comprised of a set of linkages between the sender and the receiver. The links progress hierarchically from the physical to the mental level and can be applied when there are multiple receivers or when there are disparities of time or distance between the sender and the receiver. The state of the communication at any given point is not illustrative of a Markov process but is cumulative; the entire pathway through the system of linkages influences the future or the ultimate success of the communication. An important aspect of the model is the recognition that, at each point of linkage, the phenomenon in question affects and is affected by both the sender and the receiver. Targowski and Bowman acknowledge that their effort is aimed at describing the dynamic nature of communication and criticize the 'package delivery' concept, suggesting that the package is either received or not and that it arrives either damaged or not."[26]

The mental aspects of the communication process are the more interesting and have more relevance to the human element in the library-user interchange. The models discussed so far that pay some attention to the mental side have bases founded primarily on logic. But does this capture the entirety of the mental aspect? Or is there something else that affects the process? Mickey Smith offers an alternative view:

> Let us recognize some obvious and apparent components of human communication. In any conversation between people, two channels of meaningful communication are usually open at any time: a cognitive one and an emotional one. Cognitive communication follows a logical structure, perhaps constructed along the patterns of rational language. Cognitive communication depends on the definitions of words, phrases, and

Figure 3.7
Targowski-Bowman Model of the Communication Process

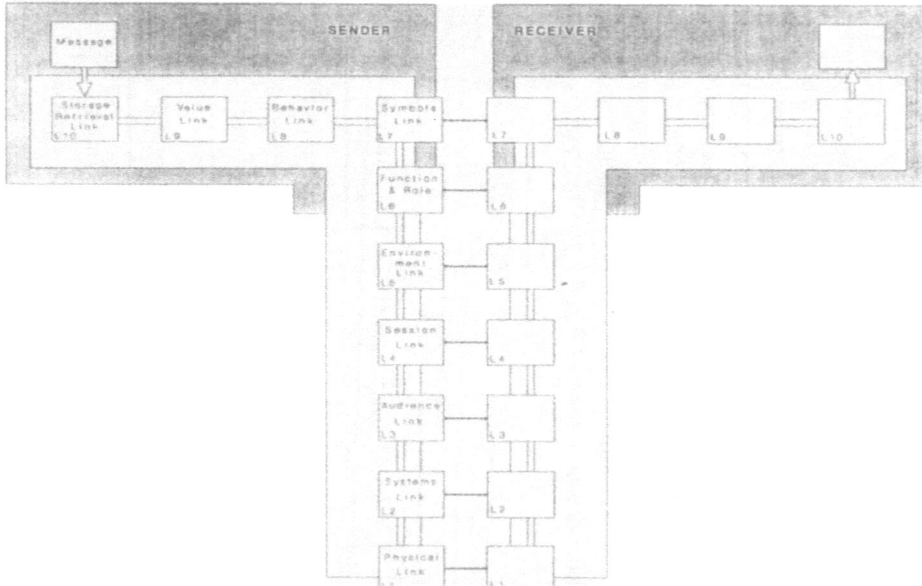

Source: Andrew S. Targowski and Joel P. Bowman, "The Layer-Based Pragmatic Model of the Communication Process," *Journal of Business Communication* Vol. 25 (Winter 1988): 11. Reprinted with permission of the authors.

sentences. It is public and understandable by almost anyone. Emotional communication may lie outside language, and may include facial gestures, voice tone, word choice, and other signs of feeling. Emotional communication carries feeling messages; cognitive communication carries more logical messages. These two messages are different in form and content. When we understand another person, we understand both of these messages and their relation to each other.[27]

His model reflects the multiple facets of human communication (see Figure 3.8). There is a parallel between his vision of communication and human information processing. Each consists of levels of activity that are not unlike neural evolution; each emerging phase makes use of what came before, building step by step to construct layers of complexity. In this manner the cognitive protocols, residing at the top of the model, use both memory and feeling to create and affirm ideas. Smith goes further with his concepts to include group memory or group knowledge. Figures 3.9 and 3.10 illustrate his notions.

Figure 3.8
Smith Model I

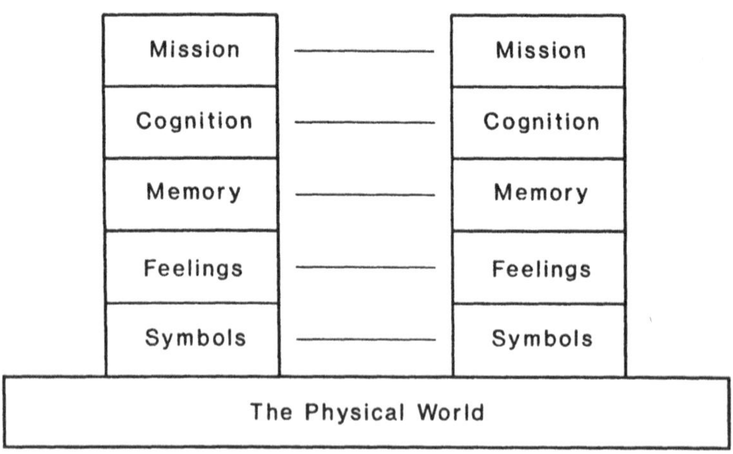

Source: Mickey Smith, "A Model of Human Communication," *IEEE Communications Magazine* 26 (February 1988): 5. © 1988 IEEE. Reprinted with permission of IEEE.

Figure 3.9
Smith Model II

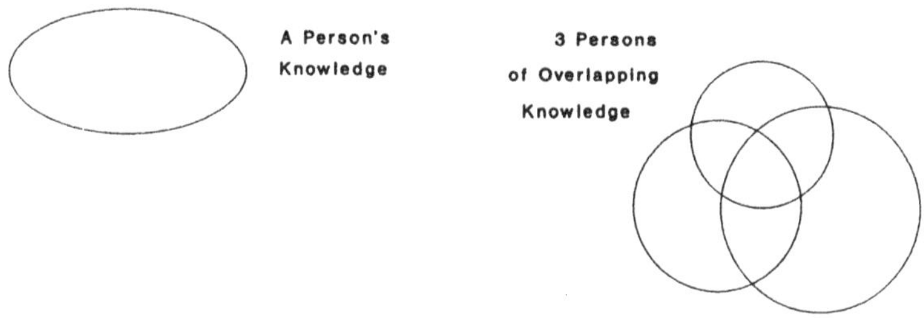

Source: Mickey Smith, "A Model of Human Communication," *IEEE Communications Magazine* 26 (February 1988): 11. © 1988 IEEE. Reprinted with permission of IEEE.

Figure 3.10
Smith Model III

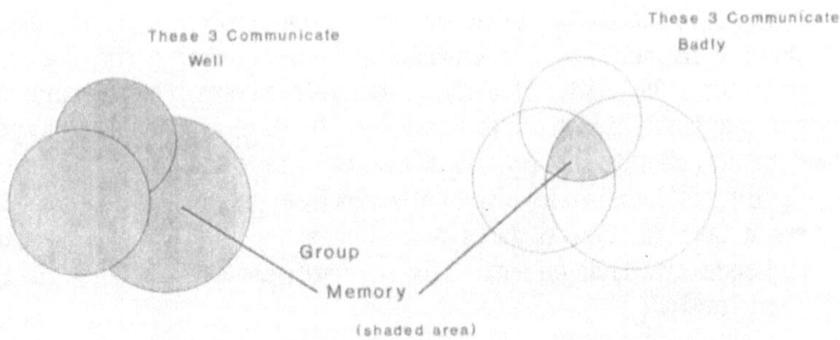

Source: Mickey Smith, "A Model of Human Communication," *IEEE Communications Magazine* 26 (February 1988): 11. © 1988 IEEE. Reprinted with permission of IEEE.

In Figure 3.10 Smith points out function and dysfunction of group memory. "Among people who communicate easily and transparently, group memory consists of all relevant knowledge of any individual, their logical union. Among groups of suspicious, reticent noncommunicators, group memory consists of only what they all agree upon, i.e. their logical intersection, which is much smaller."[28] Smith's thoughts on human communication systems have relevance to the topic at hand, which will be explored later.

One final model of import here is not really a communication model at all, but an organizational model. This concept was articulated by Michael Cohen, James March, and Johan Olsen.

> Consider organized anarchies. These are organizations—or decision situations—characterized by three general properties. The first is problematic preferences. In the organization it is difficult to impute a set of preferences to the decision situation that satisfies the standard consistency requirements for a theory of choice. The organization operates on the basis of a variety of inconsistent and ill-defined preferences. It can be described better as a loose collection of ideas than as a coherent structure; it discovers preferences through action more than it acts on the basis of preferences.
>
> The second property is unclear technology. Although the organization manages to survive and even produce, its own processes are not understood by its members. It operates on the basis of simple trial-and-error procedures, the residue of learning from the accidents of past experience, and pragmatic inventions of necessity. The third property is fluid participation. Participants vary in the amount of time and effort they devote to different domains; involvement varies from one time to another. As a result, the boundaries of the organization are uncertain and changing; the audiences and decision makers for any particular kind of choice change capriciously.[29]

The decision process in such an organization is best characterized by a garbage can in which four variables—choices, problems, potential solutions, and energy from the participants—interact, attach to, and detach from one another, not quite randomly, but based on complex behavioral phenomena. This may not be the most effective problem resolution mechanism, but, where ambiguity or conflict exist, it does enable choices to be made and some problems to be resolved. The connection of this model with communication, especially in libraries, will be grist for further discussion.

WHERE DOES INFORMATION FIT IN?

Each of the models presented has some application to the librarian–user exchange. Each also has some pertinence for the library's position in the process. The next chapters will address the functions of both library and librarian in a number of these conceptual frameworks. What is important to note at this juncture is that, if the library itself is a mechanism for communication (if it is useless if communication is not central to its activity), the elements of the models should reach the consciousness of all librarians. Anything that can enhance the productivity of the library and heighten the accomplishment of its primary purpose needs to be recognized and studied.

Beyond the library and the librarian, which will be discussed in turn, is information itself. Much of the nature of the message, inherent in the majority of the models, centers on information. Recalling the definition of information—that which informs, which gives significance to—prompts the realization that, for each communication exchange, there are limited relevant choices for appropriate messages. One difficulty for communication in a library environment is that the relevant choices are in amongst other alternatives that are not pertinent. As is evident from Chapter 2, too much information (in the generic sense) can present problems as serious as too little.

The information production mechanism is not interested in the effects of the bulk of information on each exchange. Production is aimed at specific markets, large and small. Each producer targets a market with certain needs; a given market (which may be seen as a set of receivers) has the goods of several sources to select from. Even with a simple model, it is evident that the market as receiver is approached, actively or tacitly, by multiple sources. In the same way that a person may have difficulty when more than one other person is speaking to him or her, the market for information can become confused by the noise of several messages. Since production of information is steadily increasing, even to specialized markets, the integrity of the system may be seen to be in jeopardy.

The models depicted in this chapter are designed primarily to illustrate functioning communication systems. The source selects a message, encodes it, and transmits it to a receiver, which decodes it. That is the most simplistic model. Some writers point out the fluidity of roles and other personal or environmental factors that affect, for instance, the acts of encoding and decoding. The amount of information available, though, can lead to dysfunction. At this point it is important to reiterate the concept of entropy as stated by Shannon and Weaver. If information in their terminology refers to degree of choice and is comparable to entropy in thermodynamics, the increases in the amount of information (as used elsewhere in this book) lead to more and more choices. Of course, it is impossible to discuss entropy and information outside the context of the library. The next chapter will address the ways the library assists with the process, how its organizing function facilitates the functioning of communicating (as the models suggest), and, conversely, how it may not function successfully.

NOTES

1. Ronald L. Smith, *General Models of Communication*, Special Report No. 5 (West Lafayette, IN: Purdue University, Department of Speech, 1962).
2. Karl W. Deutsch, "On Communication Models in the Social Sciences," *Public Opinion Quarterly*, 16 (1952), 357.
3. Klaus Krippendorff, "Models of Messages: Three Prototypes," in *The Analysis of Communication Content*, ed. George Gerbner and others (New York: Wiley, 1969), 101.
4. Harold D. Lasswell, "The Structure and Function of Communication in Society," in *The Communication of Ideas*, ed. Lyman Bryson (New York: Harper & Row, 1948), 37.
5. Werner J. Severin and James W. Tankard, Jr., *Communication Theories: Origins, Methods, Uses* (New York: Hastings House, 1979), 30.

6. Claude E. Shannon and Warren Weaver, *The Mathematical Theory of Communication* (Urbana: University of Illinois Press, 1949), 7, 34.

7. Charles E. Osgood, "Psycholinguistics: A Survey of Theory and Research Problems," *Journal of Abnormal and Social Psychology*, 49 (October 1954), 3.

8. Ibid.

9. Ibid.

10. Wilbur Schramm, "How Communication Works," in *The Process and Effects of Mass Communication*, ed. Wilbur Schramm and Donald Roberts (Urbana: University of Illinois Press, 1954), 22.

11. Ibid.

12. Frank E. X. Dance, "Toward a Theory of Human Communication," in *Human Communication Theory: Original Essays*, ed. Frank E. X. Dance (New York: Holt, Rinehart, and Winston, 1967), 296.

13. Ibid., 296.

14. Thomas A. Sebeok, "Coding in the Evolution of Signalling Behavior," *Behavioral Science*, 7 (October 1962), 433.

15. K. Buhler, *Sprachtheorie* (Jena: Fischer, 1934), cited in Sebeok, "Coding in the Evolution," 433–34.

16. Sebeok, "Coding in the Evolution," 433–34.

17. Robert A. Fairthorne, "Morphology of 'Information Flow'," *Journal of the Association for Computing Machinery*, 14 (October 1967), 712.

18. Ibid., 716.

19. Calvin N. Mooers, "Analysis of the Hexagon of Notification," *Journal of Documentation*, 30 (June 1974), 187.

20. Dean C. Barnlund, "A Transactional Model of Communication," in *Foundations of Communication Theory*, ed. Kenneth K. Sereno (New York: Harper & Row, 1970), 92.

21. Ibid.

22. David P. Campbell and Dale Level, "A Black Box Model of Communications," *Journal of Business Communication*, 22 (Summer 1985), 40.

23. Ibid., 39.

24. Ibid., 44.

25. Andrew S. Targowski and Joel P. Bowman, "The Layer-Based, Pragmatic Model of the Communication Process," *Journal of Business Communication*, 25 (Winter 1988), 11.

26. Ibid., 15–16.

27. Mickey Smith, "A Model of Human Communication," *IEEE Communications Magazine*, 26 (February 1988), 5.

28. Ibid., 11.

29. Michael D. Cohen, James G. March, and Johan P. Olsen, "A Garbage Can Model of Organizational Choice," *Administrative Science Quarterly*, 17 (March 1972), 1.

4

The Library in the Communication Process

"The library has been created by actual necessities in modern civilization. It is now a necessary unit in the social fabric."

Pierce Butler[1]

IS THE LIBRARY FISH OR FOWL?

Now that there are some schemata in place that attempt to explain what goes on in the process of communication, we can turn our attention to the library and how it fits in with these models. It seems most logical to begin with the simplest representation—the linear communication put forth by Shannon and Weaver in Figure 3.1. While this model seems simple, it is deceptively so, as is evident when we try to apply gross categorizations to a situation. Where, in fact, does the library fit in to this pellucid concept? In one sense the library may be seen as the information source. Many library users approach the library as such, and this may be seen in the language users employ when referring to the library. "I'm going to see what the library can tell me about this." "Why don't you check the library and see what is says?" The library becomes similar linguistically and conceptually to the idea of the computer.

It is transformed in the user's mind to an independent entity, almost a living organism capable of generating its product—information. The library behaves in some ways like other organizations—it must have an influx of resources and people to manage those resources, and it is dependent on outside forces such as the publishing industry and the size of the tax base. These rational considerations give way, though, to a nonrational view. R. K. Stamper observes (and rejects) the notion of information as a mystical fluid;[2] a similar mysticism seems to surround the idea "library," and should likewise be rejected. The discussion of this chapter will focus on the library apart from the librarian. Concentration will be on those users who, by choice or circumstance, do not interact with a person during their time spent in the library. Many users will, through avoidance or through confidence (rightly or wrongly felt), bypass the librarian.

In a more tangible sense the library can be seen as a source. The library is responsible for the creation, growth, and maintenance of its catalog (even though the cataloging copy does not, in many instances, originate locally). The library user might approach the library through its catalog, translating a conceptual need into a more concrete point of access. The user doesn't care that the catalog is not locally originated. It is based locally, so a perception of its origin is likewise locally centered. The medium of the catalog is also largely irrelevant to these considerations—card or online, the catalog is the property of, and perhaps in some ways the embodiment of, the library. This proprietary relationship is imbedded in the language we use when we speak of "the library's catalog." Efforts to transcend the local base are not new; union catalogs have existed for many years and, not infrequently, on a large scale. The largest of these is probably OCLC's Online Union Catalog. The existence of union catalogs, however, does not negate the local nature of the catalog, especially in the user's perspective.

From another perspective the library may be seen as a source in that it is responsible for the "collection." Granted, other individuals or entities are responsible for each of the works included in the collection, but the library has selected these materials—according to some conscious plan, one would hope. Therefore we speak of "the library's collection," noting a responsibility for the growth and development of the collection. Users may think in terms of "What does the library have?" There is implicit in such a view an admission, not just of ownership or proprietorship, but responsibility. It may be that some library users do not actually separate the work consulted from the library. This notion is admittedly tenuous, but so is the connection between the library and the information in it. This may be particularly true of the reference collection. If a person enters the library looking for a novel by a certain author and it is available, there is likely to be little confusion regarding the source of the words read. That source is James Michener, or Stephen King, or John Updike. If that person approaches a reference librarian to find out how much a gallon of water weighs and the answer to that query is provided by the librarian through the use of a reference book, then what, to the user's mind, is the source of the information?

The tenuousness of the connection is exacerbated when we deal with *access* to information, rather than ownership. If a library user's need is satisfied by a mediated search of a full-text database, for instance, what, to the user, is the source of information? The actual source of the information is even more transparent than when a librarian consults a printed work. If someone were to ask the user—after the fact—where the information came from, that person may well respond, "the library." Such a response would be both correct and incorrect and would rely on the perception of the individual and that person's awareness of, need for, and dependence on an ultimate source of the information. Roles can be quite fluid, especially in the perceptions of the various participants in the process.

The question that may arise in many minds is, "What difference does it make?" In a number, possibly even a majority, of instances it makes not the least difference. A user with an express need seeks only an answer to a question. Wherever that answer may be obtained is, then, the source of the answer. Suppose someone is working a crossword puzzle and comes upon the clue, "Lord what

_____ these mortals be." If a companion can supply the missing word (fools) then that person is the source of information. It matters little to the puzzler that it is a line from *A Midsummer Night's Dream*. One could wax philosophical and argue on the basis of ontological reality, but pragmatism may be argued just as strongly. The answer to the question that started this paragraph is "None," unless it matters to the person initiating the request. A student, for example, may have to attribute the information to a specific source. The users' perceptions are the effective determinants; otherwise, this is a moot point.

At some point in these exchanges between users and the library, the library also functions as a receiver. The user initiates a request by entering the library. The library anticipates some requests by providing signage directing users to various locations within the library where the exchange can continue. The library's card catalog functions in somewhat the same manner, as does the operative classification schedule. We should be careful not to make too much of this; there is only so far one can anthropomorphize an entity like a library, and only so far such an entity can go as a receiver. The function of receiver is more evident as a user approaches an interactive online catalog. Receipt of a message is more literal in such a circumstance; the user must take a more active role in initiating a message (request or search). In this scenario, the catalog responds to a request. The exchange more closely resembles a dyadic process between two humans. The same may be concluded about some compact disc products and other end-user search mechanisms, as long as one equates these and the catalog with "library." Again, individual perception will govern the perspective taken, but one function of the library in such a model is likely to arouse little dispute.

THE LIBRARY AS CHANNEL

Logic dictates that, for most information of interest in the present discussion, we look beyond the library to find the source, since the library is not usually the point of origin of information.

This identification of source is included in the library's own catalog. In catalogs there is an attempt to attribute, to credit the producer of the work whenever possible. From the catalog one can tell that John Irving wrote *The World According to Garp*. There is not likely to be, as noted above, the mistaken impression that the library is responsible for the work. In terms of the model, Irving is sending a message; the book forms the signal that is transmitted. The reader, then, is the ultimate destination of the message. The means of transmitting the message becomes complicated, though. A narrow view of channel suggests that the book (in this case, the artifact, the print on paper) is the channel, the medium by which the signal is transmitted. While this is indeed so, there is more to the means by which Irving's words reach the reader.

The publisher would have to be included as part of the channel—without a publisher there would be no transmission. The printer, who is responsible for the physical production of the artifact, functions as the transmitter, the producer of the signal. A distributor or jobber would also come into play, although there are less economical ways that can be used to bypass this element. To the reader, the publisher and the distributor are largely unseen; their roles are not readily apparent. The reader *is* aware of the medium—the physical entity identified as the book. The reader is also aware of the library as a means of receiving the signal sent by Irving via the printer. In the library user's mind and activity, the library does function as a channel over which information flows from a source to a receiver. In Shannon's structure, "The channel is merely the medium used to transmit the signal from transmitter to receiver."[3] Ignoring the problematic language of Shannon's definition, it is evident that the library functions as a linking element in the communication process.

Moreover, the library contains certain mechanisms designed to improve or enhance its function as a channel. The most important and most basic is the library's catalog. This mechanism is fairly obvious; a library user may have expectations that certain titles will be held or that certain information will be available, but cannot *know* this to be so until an intervening tool, the catalog, verifies it.

Further, verification of holdings is not sufficient; some indication of access is needed. The classification schedule allows a user to find the objects sought. Classification also assists the library's channel function by providing a link based on physical proximity. Like items are placed together in the schemes of the widely-used classification systems. On the face of it, cataloging and classification appear to make the library an efficient channel. The process should be able to proceed apace and signal transmission should flow smoothly. Is this, in fact, the case?

As was noted earlier, communication as a phenomenon has many purposes. A number of its purposes are intentional; some are not. Intentional purposes seek to strengthen the probability of a desired potential outcome. One such purpose is information. (We are stricken again by the multivalent nature of our language; ideation, in the instance of "information," has outrun articulation.) The library, as a communication device or entity, seeks to inform (see the definition in Chapter 2). This intention does not guarantee success. Wilbur Schramm notes that "the process of informational communication requires four steps—four hurdles to be cleared: (1) to attract attention to it, (2) to have it accepted, (3) to have it interpreted and—so the communicator hopes—(4) stored away for later use."[4] The first step carries its own implications, which will not be dealt with here. In actuality step three should precede step two. Acceptance cannot come before interpretation, and interpretation, for the library, is not a simple matter.

The discussion of meaning, a couple of chapters ago, touches on the difficulty of language and the importance of language sharing to meaning formation. Essentially what the library does through its cataloging and classification practices is to create a language, a code that the key to the utility of the library, its contents, and access beyond its walls. The typical library user does not instinctively know about this code. Knowledge of the code cannot be taken for granted, but in many libraries it effectively is. If the library is to function as a communication channel, it should not create impediments to the signal flow. More will be said about this later.

Other complicating factors to be dealt with in examining the library as channel are the information itself and the information needs of users. If we use the Shannon and Weaver concept of information as freedom of choice, and freedom of choice is akin to entropy, then the library is a highly entropic system. This would be true if all information in a library were equal when it comes to responding to a specific need, but the set of potentially relevant information (I_r) is a small subset of available information (I): $I_r \in I$. Entropy is in one sense reduced, but only if the user can limit I to I_r. A user's success at limiting the set is dependent, first, on his or her ability to define the information need in sufficiently explicit terms such that a clear concept of the need emerges and, second, on the ability to translate that need into terms operational in the library (subject headings, segments of the classification schedule, index terms, etc.). The language problems noted above arise again as a potential specter haunting the user.

The retrieval task is further complicated by the propensity for complexity in many library searches. While the simplest form of information is binary (yes or no), the information sought by library users is more dynamical and so is not simple. Part of the problem is the potentially large number of possibilities, especially with a less-than-well-defined request, which itself decreases the chances of success. The library, as an element in the communication process, does some amount of pre-selection through the use of subject headings and classification. If we are limited to a library–user dyad, though, success will be limited by the ability, or inability of the user to recognize a correct response or "good" information. The library is unable to assist such recognition beyond the provision of pre-selected aids that may serve as cues or checks.

Though it seems obvious, the library is limited (or has opportunities) based on the other aspects of communication channels previously discussed. As a channel, the library has a difficult time transcending the media available. The producers of information—book and periodical publishers, video and database producers, for example—supply the marketplace with products. They do not supply the content; authors, film-makers, and others are responsible for that. They do package the content for sale, though. These media will influence the library, to the extent that both physical and intellectual access is provided. When Marshall McLuhan wrote that "the medium is the message," he meant that "the personal and social consequences of any medium—that is, any extension of ourselves—result from the new scale that is introduced into our affairs by each extension of ourselves, or by any new technology."[5] If changes in media alter consequences for humans, they do so for libraries as well. A different medium will be approached differently; in fact, it may demand to be approached differently. What results may be like staring at the face of a digital watch, wondering which way is counterclockwise.

To give a cursory illustration of the differences in media, let us look at one possible error that may occur with the library as channel. Suppose a library owns a book that a user is looking for and the book is on the shelf in its assigned spot. The main entry card, however, is misfiled in the card catalog. If the user does not search the catalog in places where the main entry card does *not* belong, the person may be led to believe that the library does not have the book. The user might get lucky and find the book by browsing the stacks, but that is an iffy proposition. An online catalog may help the library be a better channel, since rules of filing need not hamper a search. Suppose, though, that the user misspells the author's name. The same frustration as above may result, or the online system may permit browsing if there is no direct match in the database. Of course other types of errors can plague users of online catalogs, but this example illustrates that different media allow, or even necessitate, different modes of use.

A definite concern with any communication channel is the capacity of the channel. All channels have finite capacity but technology now allows a very large capacity for some technical channels. Fiber optics, for instance, has resulted in substantial increases in voice and data capacity. The capacity of a library as a channel is also finite, and is dependent on some tangible, even mundane, factors. Some libraries may be limited by the size of the physical facility. A building can hold only so much stuff; when it is filled, a dilemma arises. When there is no more room in a small library, a common policy is to remove an item for every new item added. This retains a dynamic aspect of the library, but growth is certainly restricted. This is not necessarily bad; the library user may benefit from the acquisition of new material while not having to deal with the potentially higher entropy brought about by a greater number of choices. The drawback is having to decide what to remove.

The size factor is not limited to small libraries; large facilities are finite as well. The largest research library has a limited capacity and that capacity will someday be reached. Many large libraries are reluctant to weed as they add. The result is a greater number of choices and a greater possibility of entropy. One response by libraries is to use remote storage facilities. This in some ways controls freedom of choice in the central facility; it may result in a relatively constant collection size in that building. The catalog, however, continues to grow, which still presents problems for the user. The implications for a card catalog are obvious; the growth is visible. Suppose someone approaches an online catalog, though, and searches for works on chromothermodynamics. If there are 437 hits on that term, the problem of choice stares the user in the face. There is the possibility of linking another term with the original to limit choice. Can we trust the language of the catalog enough to believe that by so doing both precision and recall will be high?

Money is another feature of channel capacity relevant to libraries. The capacity is limited by the extent of available financial resources. The reality of scale that applies to space also applies to fiscal matters. A small library is going to have a relatively small budget, which will allow limited growth. Larger libraries will have more money, but one effect of the more ample financial resources is an increase in the choices available.

The connection between channel capacity and freedom of choice is a problematic one for libraries. If information sources are considered to be the myriad producers of books, periodicals, videos, databases, and other media, then the capacity of the channel (library) is going to be constricted by the reality of space, money, and time. A library user may enter a library seeking a discrete signal—a hot best-seller. If the library does not have that title available, there is a channel failure and the communication process cannot be completed successfully. If the request is for a less discrete signal—a book on starting a small business—there may be a better chance for success. The library does not operate in the same way as a channel that has a capacity for x number of signals in an environment of limited signal transmission, or periodic signal transmission, such as a telephone system. The signal transmission in the library setting (that is, the production of information) is vast in type and number and not of brief or determined duration. Even a lengthy telephone call may last only a couple of hours; at the end of the call the signal is no longer transmitted. The channel is then able to handle another call. The demand for certain information may last for years; as long as that demand lasts, the channel's capacity is affected. The library can broaden its capacity to an extent by putting resources into access as opposed to ownership. This action will be productive for some kinds of information, but not all.

The dilemma for libraries is the recognition that there will be a large discrepancy between the number of signals transmitted and the capacity of the channel. Libraries have tried to solve this by expanding the definition of channel and its capacity. The channel ceases to be one library, one physical facility, and the stuff in it. Interlibrary loan is perhaps the most basic example of this effort. The holdings of other libraries may be used to complete the communication transaction. Union lists, cooperative collection development, and shared databases are further examples of libraries' attempts to envision the channel more as the community of libraries. These endeavors have been effective to the extent that the user is patient enough with the process. Document delivery, telefacsimile, and improved technical communication have helped bolster user confidence. These measures can only go so far, though. As improvements in the channel are made, user expectations are heightened. If the library of the future becomes largely, if not wholly, electronic, it will do so in part because it results in improvements in channel capacity and performance.

Capacity, as a delimiter, is not confined to the channel; it also applies to the receiver. Some have manipulated a bit of role reversal and have referred to the "channel capacity" of the receiver. George Miller states that this "represents the greatest amount of information that he [the receiver or, as it applies here, the library user] can give us about the stimulus. . . . The channel capacity is the upper limit to which the observer can match his responses to the stimuli we give him."[6] There is only so much that an individual can absorb, only so much of even that which informs that can be taken and assimilated. Part of this limitation is a function of capacity, part of the disequilibrium of an individual's capacity and that of the channel. One manifestation of the dysfunction is overload, but more on that when we get to "noise."

One concept of the communication channel and its function provides a link between the library as channel and the library as source. Fred Dretske writes,

> The channel of communication = that set of existing conditions (on which the signal depends) that either (1) generate no (relevant) information, or (2) generate only redundant information (from the point of view of the receiver). . . . This is why a signal, though depending on conditions both at the source and on the channel, carries information about *only* the source. Among the conditions on which the signal depends, *only the source* is a generator of new information [italics in original].[7]

If the library, then, were strictly and solely a channel in this narrow sense it would be all but unusable. Materials would be placed in the building haphazardly with no indication where anything might be found. The library's utility depends on its role as source in providing a means of access to the signals of other sources.

THE LIBRARY IN OTHER MODELS

The above exposition focuses on the linear communication model of Shannon and Weaver and how the library fits in as a multifaceted element. There are, as we have seen, other iterations of the communication model, and the library–user relationship can be seen in those terms as well. The linear model was dealt with first because of the difficulty (but not impossibility) of interaction between the user and the library. To a considerable extent, interaction depends on how forgiving the library is able to be. As was mentioned previously, some online catalogs include means of getting around problems of spelling, at least insofar as they may offer the user other options. Card catalogs and other aspects of the library as a retrieval mechanism and as a channel are far less forgiving. The user might wander into a circular dilemma similar to being told to consult a dictionary to find a word he or she cannot spell.

In such a circumstance there is a breakdown at the physical level; the user is unable to interpret what the library offers in its role of either source or channel. Harkening back to the model proposed by Targowski and Bowman, such a failure indicates dysfunction at the lowest, most elemental link. Dysfunction at that level usually prevents the process from moving any further. In practical terms, to borrow from the language of queuing theory, what is likely to occur is reneging—the user may well terminate the process out of frustration. Further, that individual will be reluctant to consult a system that does not or cannot allow for compensating difficulties at the physical level, especially if the person is conditioned by other systems equipped with such compensation ability.

At a simple level, derived from the linear model, the success of any transaction is dependent, as Schramm noted, on the overlapping fields of experience of the source and the destination. Both the encoding and decoding of a signal are germane to the notion of overlapping experience or awareness. The library has been criticized in the past for not paying attention to what the user brings to the process. "The library is organized for its own convenience" would be a paraphrase of some of that criticism. Inherent in this attitude is an accusation that libraries ignore the user, the user's knowledge base, vocabulary, and cognitive processes. It is the user's responsibility to conform to the library. A further condemnation asserts that the library sees itself as largely immutable; it does not change, other things must adapt to its structure. Of course the harshest of this kind of criticism is overstated, but there is more than a grain of truth to the more moderate articulation of stricture. A recognition of this kind of dysfunction, both real and potential, would aid in creating a more sensitive environment for the fostering of community.

The notions put forth by Schramm are implicit in the levels of protocols Smith observes. It is an easy matter to recognize the verbal protocols in library–user transactions. The encoding and decoding of the vocabularies used by each are essential to success. At another level, the importance of cognitive protocols should also be acknowledged. Smith has this set of protocols at the highest level, but, for the purpose of discussion here, perhaps they belong at the lowest levels. Even more fundamental than the verbal protocols are the concepts underlying information, its structure, and its use. The library user has to recognize and accept, for instance, that the physical arrangement of a library has to be linear. An item can occupy only one location at a time and it is not feasible for the library to provide multiple copies at multiple locations. It should be recognized by *both* the user and the library that it is at least part of the function of the catalog to transcend the linearity of physical space.

Unfortunately, but inevitably, there are opposite forces at work. The user and the library embody what George K. Zipf describes as the Force of Diversification and the Force of Unification.[8] According to such a notion, the effort of the user is most efficiently conserved by the Force of Diversification if each and every word, term, or sign (in the semiotic sense) has an unambiguous and unique meaning and usage. If this were the case there would be no worries about dual meaning, equivocation, or dubious usage of language. The effort of the library, on the other hand, would be most efficiently conserved by the Force of Unification if all possible means and usages could be conveyed by a single word. Naturally some degree of compromise is required, and language is such that it allows ambiguity. In practical application, it would be more helpful if the library were aware of the Force of Diversification and made efforts to incorporate its premise into the library's language. This may mean attempting to increase the level of redundancy. Remember Schramm's hurdles that must be cleared in information communication. He points out that in telegrams, for example, certain words such as the word "not," are repeated to minimize the chance of misinterpretation. He also observes, "Once the message has been encoded as well as possible and offered where it is likely to attract attention, then the sender can do little more except be alert to the feedback from the receiver."[9]

The compromise necessary suggests that the relationship between the library and the user is conscious on both parts. There is an ideal, at least on the part of the library, that exists for use. In fact, the library does not exist for itself; the majority of institutions are open to the public. S. R. Ranganathan, who put forth five laws of library science, did not write, "Books are for hording." It is not meaningless to ask if preservation, taken to the extreme and precluding use entirely, is at all worthwhile. Preserving items so that they may be used long into the future is an admirable and necessary goal of libraries. Walter M. Miller's speculative vision in *A Canticle for Leibowitz* may not be so far removed from actuality, though. He writes,

> Brother Librarian groaned as yet another lead-sealed cask was rolled out of storage for unsealing. Armbruster was not impressed by the fact that the secular scholar, in two days, had unraveled a bit of a puzzle that had been lying around, a complete enigma, for a dozen centuries. To the custodian of the Memorabilia, each unsealing represented another decrease in the probable lifetime of the contents of the cask, and he made no attempt to conceal his disapproval of the entire proceeding. To Brother Librarian, whose task in life was the preservation of books, the principle reason for the existence of books was that they might be preserved perpetually. Usage was secondary, and to be avoided if it threatened longevity.[10]

In *Canticle*, information, so preserved, was useless; nothing meaningful could be inferred from it.

The perception of meaning is implied throughout the model of Campbell and Level. It is more of a condensation of what occurs within a communication transaction and, at various stages along the way, there is the opportunity for symbolic interpretation. The model emphasizes that while a message is sent from a source to a destination, meaning resides elsewhere. Walter Coutu says,

> meaning is not an entity, it has no locus; it is something that occurs rather than exists. Meaning does not inhere in things or words, but in sign behavior. . . . Despite our Aristotelian thought forms nothing in the universe "has" meaning, but anything may become a stimulus to evoke meaning by way of inducing the percipient to give self instructions on how to behave in relation to it.[11]

The complexity of the library's position in the communication process may be especially evident in the models of Sebeok, Fairthorne, and Mooers. All three focus on a particular structure of elements that gives rise almost naturally to the identification of triadic relationships. Just as with the linear model, the library may be seen as source or channel, and focus on one or the other will determine the library's place in the various relationships. The simplest relationship, as is shown in Fairthorne's depiction, is the routing function of the channel between the source and the destination. The most problematic may be that of linguistic accord between the source and destination in transmitting a message. It is with such a function, though, that the emphasis on triads becomes less satisfactory. It is difficult to admit to the need for linguistic accord without taking into account the code that the source uses to create the message. Examining triads is useful for seeking the explanation for the operational aspects of communication elements, but Fairthorne and Mooers suggest that relational interaction in the communication process is even more complex.

Some of the complexity of the library's role in communication is suggested by the application of Smith's models. He writes of the potential for knowledge expansion when individuals pool their knowledge bases. If the concept of group memory functions well there is more effective communication and an opportunity to expand the horizon of any one individual. A similar scheme could be applied to the library community. For instance, if access beyond the holdings of any single library (which is certainly technologically feasible) is a reality, there is an analogy to multiple persons with overlapping knowledge. In fact, the overlap can extend beyond libraries as institutions to other agencies or other information storage and retrieval mechanisms. Figure 4.1 illustrates this kind of overlapping relationship.

This could possibly give the patron more complete access to the information environment. Of course, dysfunction is also possible. Despite technological capability, economics may preclude the melding of resources and access into an operating network. It may be perceived that the cost is not worth the benefit. Also, success depends on organizational cooperation; the potential for communication dysfunction is even greater than for simple dyadic interaction. Agreement, which is central to success in Smith's scheme, is difficult at best to come by.

Agreement is also part of the implied functioning of the garbage can model. A version of the garbage can model with elements relevant to communication is presented in Figure 4.2. In the larger information environment the library may be seen as just one of many channels that may be used by an individual with an information need. If the library is selected, for whatever reason, as the suitable channel, other possibilities remain with regard to the message received, the referents applied by a person at a given time, and the interpretation resulting from the combination of the above. An experienced library user is likely to have a more clearly defined and more applicable set of referents to employ when selecting the library as channel. The infrequent library user is likely to apply referents from other situations and other structures, some of which will fit and some will not. Likewise, the potential messages present a problematic set of choices. The library itself may also be viewed as the garbage can. This narrower application of the model simplifies the user's dilemma only a little. The difficulty with referents, for instance, remains, as does the problem of potential messages. The selection of possible channels is somewhat more

Figure 4.1
Examples of Institutional and Informational Overlap

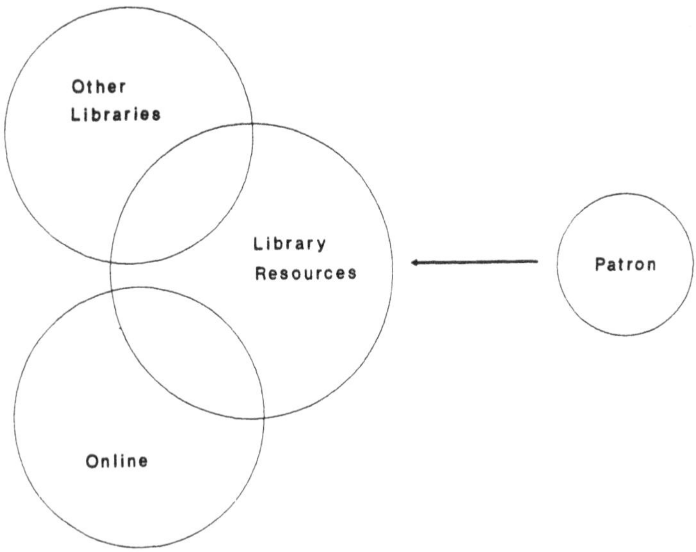

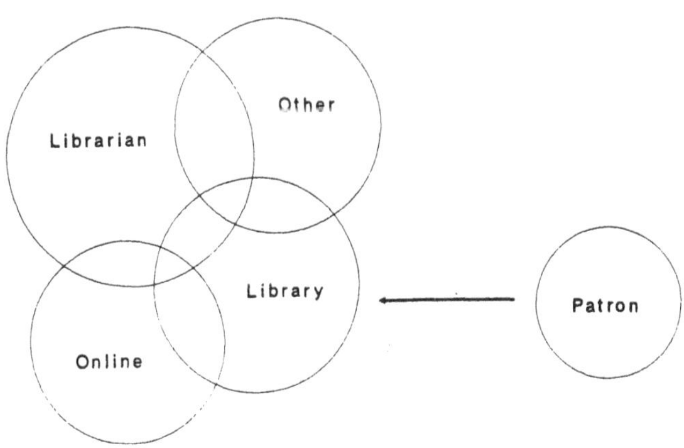

Figure 4.2
Garbage Can Model Applied to Communication

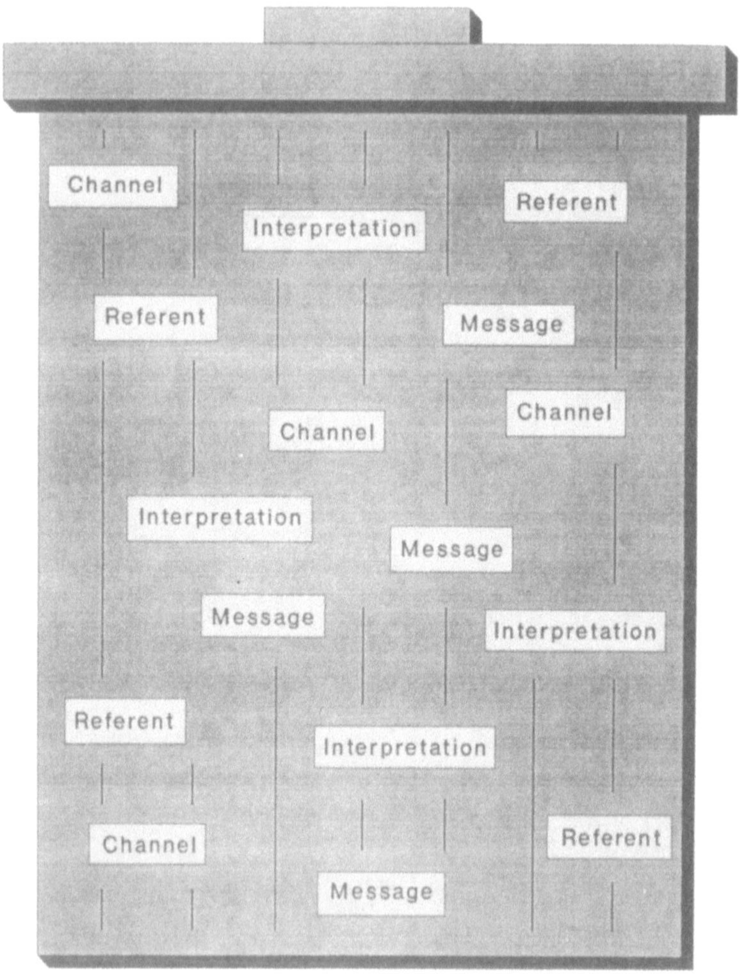

limited, and that limitation may exert a normative influence over the other variables. The possibilities are still diverse, though, and, as with the other models, there is always the possibility that things could go awry.

THE LIBRARY AS A MASS MEDIUM

We tend to think of the positive connotations of communication. We may take an ideological posture and, conditioned by the likes of Leo Buscaglia, Oprah Winfrey, and Phil Donahue, assume that the communication process invariably involves sharing. David Sless, however, notes that

> sharing, which is often assumed to be a *necessary* and defining characteristic of communication, may not be so. There is no set of universally agreed conditions that can ensure that the relation between sender and receiver in communication will involve sharing. . . . [W]*e should not take for granted the idea that communication involves sharing; rather we should always ask, in any instance, whether sharing is actually taking place* [italics in original].[12]

The library is not in an optimum position for sharing. It interacts little on a one-to-one basis with the library user. This should not be surprising; how many organizations can so interact with their clienteles?

As a mass medium, the library can only share so much with the user. The potential is not as limited as it is with such media as television, radio, or film, but since a library has a sizable population to serve it must construct a rather generic means of access. Because of this reality the user may have to meet the library more than halfway; the library will not have the flexibility to alter itself for each individual. These observations illustrate some of the differences between mass media and genuine dyadic communication—differences that are further and more succinctly articulated in tabular form by Everett Rogers,[13] Rogers's table shows how each channel handles such things as message flow, communication context, feedback, speed to the audience, and effect of the communication.

Some aspects of mass media are directly evident in an examination of the library; others, though, are less applicable or require a bit of reinterpretation in order to fit. Several aspects are expressed as assumptions by Harvey Jassem and Roger Jon Desmond; many of these can be viewed in the context of the library.[14] The first assumption is that the audience is passive, that attendance to media is more dependent on habit than on the content of the message. The library's audience has at least some opportunity to engage in some interaction with the library, although such interaction is by no means required. Habit may, in fact, play some part in the use of libraries. The passivity of the audience may be due, in part, to another assumption—delayed feedback, or the time it takes for the audience to respond to a message. Again, this may be less pronounced in the library, but some degree of user frustration may be caused by an inability to find a ready outlet for questions or comments. In the vast majority of libraries there is some effort to provide such an outlet, but the bureaucratic structure of the organization may not make this easy.

Another assumption is that of simultaneous reach, the ability of the medium to be available to its audience at about the same time. While this is true, generally, of broadcast media, it does not hold well for print media. A consumer chooses when he or she will buy a book or a magazine. The same behavior is indicative of some electronic media, such as database access. This phenomenon is more descriptive of the nature of the library as a mass medium. If the point made by Jassem and Desmond is stretched, then the library does determine availability since it sets its own schedule. The library as channel is somewhat analogous to the video cassette recorder, though, in that each frees the consumer from the constraints or availability established by the producer. From the standpoint of the producer, automation—particularly the online public access catalog—approaches the concept of simultaneous reach. Availability, locally or via remote access, is determined by the library. The idea of simultaneous reach, however, is being rendered more problematic by technology and an audience that is less willing to acquiesce to an externally-imposed schedule.

With most mass media the receivers of the signal are anonymous. The author is not familiar with all the readers; the broadcaster does not know the viewers. Also, the audience itself shares an anonymity; individuals usually do not know one another and do not act collectively. Library users, though, generally present a heterogeneous group, each with an individual need. Insofar as they deal with the library only, users focus on whatever brought them to the library. In this way they behave in much the same way as a person who reads a book or sees a movie; the experience is a personal one and the reaction to the stimulus of the medium is largely individual.

Yet another assumption is one that is somewhat related to the preceding one. Since people use the media for individual need, these audience members are able to articulate the functions media serve for them. This utilitarian notion of media is based on a suggestion that individuals are able to evaluate their own needs and to assess the offerings of the media in terms of meeting those needs. Jassem and Desmond write, "One of the most important implications of this assumption is that media operate in their lives and that people deliberately choose media to gratify needs they can specify."[15] This thinking is applicable to libraries, but only to a certain extent. People have many reasons for using a library; sometimes the reasons are specific and explicit. One person may want a particular novel by Larry McMurtry; another may want to find a state statute regarding certain commercial transactions. These individuals enter the library for these reasons with the expectation that the library will have utility for them.

On the other hand, some library users have nebulous notions of what they want from the institution. Their needs are not sufficiently formulated or articulated for the potential utility of the library to be realized. Many times the cause for the uncertainty is a lack of understanding of the information structure generally—how information is produced, how it is packaged and distributed, and how the library deals with it. There is also, in any library's community, that substantial portion of the population that is unaware of the capabilities of the library as medium. The popular view is frequently a narrow one, born of past experience and fostered by social stereotype. Marketing of the library is a fairly recent development. This activity still lags far behind that of other mass media, but is likely to become more and more essential to the formation of choice by the user.

One last assumption discussed here is the audience's concern with the effects of receiving a message as that audience influences the acquisition of knowledge and changes in behavior and attitude. This was discussed to some extent in a previous chapter, but not so much from the user's perspective. In adding to knowledge a person usually has to put information into a context. Carl Martin Allwood suggests that this involves categorizing the information to assist interpretation. He observes,

> That the human being categorizes information is fundamental for her ability to form knowledge. Categorization of stimuli means that a mapping is made between the new information and the memory representations of different concepts that the perception processes of the individual have access to. The information retrieved from memory in this way can then contribute when inferences are made, for example, further categorizations of the stimuli or of the greater totality that the stimuli is part of, i.e. the retrieved information can help to create new knowledge and conceptions.[16]

The library user is assisted in this endeavor by the library's cataloging and classification. To the user, some connections are made *a priori*; this can be a time-saving mechanism and can also be used as a cognitive device allowing the user to go beyond these connections, which are often at a surface level, to some more subtle and complex relationships.

In considering the library as an aid to knowledge formation it is important to reflect one more time on the library's language. Ferdinand de Saussure states, "Language is a system of signs that express ideas, and is therefore comparable to writing, to the deaf-mute alphabet, to symbolic rites, to codes of good manners, to military signals, etc."[17] The library's language is the means by which the purposes and activities of organization and mediation are communicated to the user. More specifically, the library is a sign, "something which stands to somebody for something in some respect or capacity,"[18] as C. S. Peirce says. For the sign to be comprehensible, the receiver or interpreter must have sufficient referents to make a cognitive link. John Kelly states the relationship thusly: "The success or failure, the quality of a communicative transaction depends, in the first place, on how completely the interpreter apprehends the sign or symbol offered by the communicator."[19] This is, naturally, going to be limited. If the sign presented by the library is recognizable, if it does not diverge drastically from other languages, codes, and signs known to the library user, there is a better chance for success. The more alien the sign, the more difficult the interpretation.

Through all of this it is important to remember that one of the manifestations of the library as a mass medium is as a transmitter of culture. Here culture is used in its broadest sense, not simply meaning "high culture" or elitism. In this capacity the library shares with other media some functions and dysfunctions. These are recognized by Stephen Littlejohn and are presented in Table 4.1.[20] The functions of the library as a mass communicator operate insofar as the library is used. In a community the public library, for example, is not used by the entire population and that subpopulation using the library is not likely to be a cross-section of the whole community. The extent of socialization that may occur as a result of the library's presence is limited by the extent of use by various segments of the community. Of course, this limited use can itself be a dysfunction. It is incumbent upon libraries to assess themselves critically and ask if the use patterns are of their own doing or if there are other social factors influencing use. Although it is not grist for discussion here, the issue of demand-based collection building should be a part of this assessment.

The library, then, has a multifarious place in the communication structure. Its function is not immutable; its participation is more

Table 4.1
Partial Functional Inventory for Mass Communications

	SYSTEM UNDER CONSIDERATION			
	SOCIETY	INDIVIDUAL	SPECIFIC SUBGROUP (E.G. POLITICAL ELITE)	CULTURE
1. Mass-communicated activity: surveillance (news)				
Functions (manifest and latent)	Warning: Natural dangers Attack; war	Warning Instrumental	Instrumental: Information useful to power	Aids cultural contact Aids cultural growth
	Instrumental: News essential to the economy and other institutions	Adds prestige: Opinion leadership	Detects: Knowledge of subverssive and deviant behavior	
	Ethicizing	Status conferral	Manages public opinion: Monitors Controls	
			Legitimizes power: Status conferral	
Dysfunctions (manifest and latent)	Threatens stability: News of "better" societies Fosters panic	Anxiety Privatization Apathy Narcotization	Threatens power: News of reality "Enemy" propoganda Exposés	Permits cultural invasion
2. Mass-communicated activity: correlation (editorial selection, interpretation, and prescription)				
Functions (manifest and latent)	Aids mobilization	Provides efficiency: Assimilating news	Helps preserve power	Impedes cultural invasion Maintains cultural consensus
	Impedes threats to social stability	Impedes: Overstimulation Anxiety Apathy Privatization		
	Impedes panic			
Dysfunctions (manifest and latent)	Increases social conformism: Impedes social change if social criticism is avoided	Weakens critical faculties	Increase responsibility	Impedes cultural growth
		Increases passivity		

	SYSTEM UNDER CONSIDERATION			
	SOCIETY	INDIVIDUAL	SPECIFIC SUBGROUP (E.G. POLITICAL ELITE)	CULTURE
3. Mass-communicated activity: cultural transmission				
Functions (manifest and latent)	Increases social cohesion: Widens base of common norms, experiences, etc. Reduces anomie Continues socialization: Reaches adults even after they have left such institutions as school	Aids integration: Exposure to common norms Reduces idiosyncrasy Reduces anomia	Extends power: Another agency for socialization	Standardizes Maintains cultural consensus
Dysfunctions (manifest and latent)	Augments "mass" society	Depersonalizes acts of socialization		Reduces variety of subcultures
4. Mass-communicated activity: entertainment				
Functions (manifest and latent)	Respite for masses	Respite	Extends power: Control over another area of life	
Dysfunctions (manifest and latent)	Diverts public: Avoids social action	Increases passivity Lowers "tastes" Permits escapism		Weakens aesthetics: "Popular culture"

Source: From *Theories of Human Communication*, Second Edition, by Stephen W. Littlejohn. © 1983 by Wadsworth, Inc. Reprinted by permission of the publisher.

fluid and depends, to a considerable extent, on the user. Nonetheless, the library attempts to present itself for use through a formal code that defines access. The code is of human construction, but the human element has a much greater role to play, as we will see shortly.

NOTES

1. Pierce Butler, *Introduction to Library Science* (Chicago: University of Chicago Press, Phoenix Books, 1961), xi.
2. R. K. Stamper, "Information: Mystical Fluid or a Subject for Scientific Inquiry?" *Computer Journal*, 28, no. 3 (1985), 194–99.
3. Claude E. Shannon and Warren Weaver, *The Mathematical Theory of Communication* (Urbana: University of Illinois Press, 1949), 34.
4. Wilbur Schramm, "The Nature of Communication Between Humans," in *The Process and Effects of Mass Communication*, rev. ed., ed. Wilbur Schramm and Donald F. Roberts (Urbana: University of Illinois Press, 1971), 38.
5. Marshall McLuhan, *Understanding Media* (New York: McGraw-Hill, 1964), 7.
6. George A. Miller, "The Magical Number Seven, Plus or Minus Two: Some Limits on Our Capacity for Processing Information," *Psychological Review*, 63 (March 1956), 82.
7. Fred I. Dretske, *Knowledge and the Flow of Information* (Cambridge: Massachusetts Institute of Technology Press, 1981), 115.
8. George K. Zipf, *Human Behavior and the Principle of Least Effort* (New York: Addison Wesley, 1949).
9. Schramm, "The Nature of Communication," 39.
10. Walter M. Miller, *A Canticle for Leibowitz* (New York: Bantam, 1961), 161.
11. Walter Coutu, "An Operational Definition of Meaning," *Quarterly Journal of Speech*, 48 (February 1962), 64.
12. David Sless, *In Search of Semiotics* (Totowa, NJ: Barnes & Noble Books, 1986), 29.
13. Everett M. Rogers, "Mass Media and Interpersonal Communication," in *Handbook of Communication*, ed. Ithiel de Sola Pool (New York: Houghton Mifflin, 1973), 291.
14. Harvey C. Jassem and Roger Jon Desmond, "Mass Communication Theory and the New Media: Major Assumptions in Light of Technological Change," in *Information and Behavior*, vol. 1, ed. Brent D. Ruben (New Brunswick, NJ: Transaction Books, 1985), 130–34.

15. Ibid., 134.
16. Carl Martin Allwood, "Anthropology of Knowledge and Cognitive Psychology," *Communication & Cognition*, 20, no. 4 (1987), 299.
17. Ferdinand de Saussure, *Course in General Linguistics* (New York: McGraw-Hill, 1966), 16.
18. Charles S. Peirce, *Collected Papers, 1931–1935* (Cambridge, MA: Harvard University Press, 1931), vol. 5, 484.
19. John C. Kelly, *A Philosophy of Communication* (London: Centre for the Study of Communication and Culture, 1981), 123.
20. Stephen W. Littlejohn, *Theories of Human Communication*, 2d ed. (Belmont, CA: Wadsworth Publishing Company, 1983), 286–87.

5

The Librarian in the Communication Process

THE HUMAN ELEMENT

The previous chapter may give an impression of the library as an automaton. The discussion of the library as an entity is not intended to seem either mechanistic or deterministic, but to point out that, to many library users, the library takes on the impersonal, perhaps even monolithic, characteristics of some social organizations. The library is, of course, a human creation. From those ancient libraries mentioned in the first chapter to the myriad manifestations of library today, building and maintaining libraries are decidedly human endeavors that spring from a desire and a need to preserve and communicate human thought. That thought may be mundane; it may be data regarding land use, weather patterns, economic trends, and so forth. It may transcend data and aim at assimilation and explanation—why a certain war began or what particle is the most elemental in nature. It may attempt creation—a unique vision of society, a fictional look at human relationships, a dramatization of events real or imaginary.

The above statement that libraries serve to preserve human thought may be criticized by some members of the library community. It is true that the emphasis of an individual library may not be preservation; there simply are not sufficient resources for that to be a realistic goal. Nonetheless, the library does serve a preservation function, and that function is essential to the library's communication imperative. The function is evident in some activities of networks, in interlibrary loan, in shared bibliographic databases. In the context of Chapter 4, this serves the purpose of increasing the channel's capacity, of making more information potentially available.

The notions of purpose and function do not result from any mechanism, any automata. They are based on human activity. The library's catalog, collection, and organization (physical and intellectual) are human creations. Yet when a library user seeks information in a library there may be no direct human contact, even though that person is making use of the apparatus designed by librarians. In this way, as was stated in the preceding chapter, the library acts as a mass medium. This chapter focuses on the librarian as that person communicates directly with the library user.

This phenomenon is interpersonal communication—something different from organizational or mass communication, although elements of interpersonal communication are essential to those other manifestations. Much of the previous chapters is relevant here: the importance of shared language, signs and their interpretation, concepts of information. Some differences exist, though, between the user–library communication discussed previously and the usual dyadic user–librarian communication of interest here. The latter forms a discourse in the sense of an exchange between two individuals. The success of the discourse depends in part on coherence. This, Marilyn Merritt says,

> might be conceptualized as follows: from the point of view of the speaker, coherence is achieved through the sequencing of sentences or sentence-like units. . . . with this constraint: each sentence must be selected and placed so as to show its relevance to the ones that have occurred earlier in the sequence. From the point of view of the interpreter the relevance of the notion is not in achieving coherence, but rather in understanding

or analyzing it. For this, the selection and placement procedure can be reversed. Each sentence in a coherent discourse can be assumed to be *interpretable*, and can be examined for the achievement of that interpretability.[1]

A question arises: To what extent are the library user and the librarian aware of the importance of coherence? In one way or another, coherence is a part of virtually every librarian's education. It is the essential thrust of the interview with the user, which is built on the principle of feedback. The librarian first assumes the role of interpreter as the user begins the query. The roles then switch as the librarian seeks to clarify or verify what the user has requested. As attention turns to the place of the librarian in communication models this phenomenon will be explored further.

During the librarian–user exchange forces work simultaneously in favor of and in opposition to communication. These are variations on the forces recognized by Zipf. From the standpoint of the interpreter (whoever is acting in that role at the time) the operant dynamic may be seen as the Force of Clarity. The listener (or reader in some cases) wants to receive a message that is unambiguous and unequivocal, that has a very low probability of misinterpretation. Then the listener can be assured that he or she understands the message and can act on the basis of that understanding. From the standpoint of the speaker, though, behavior may be more heavily influenced by the Force of Ambiguity. There can be several reasons for this. One may be a lack of cognitive directedness, an unclear notion of what is being asked or said. For instance, a library user with a vague idea of a paper topic for school may introduce as much ambiguity as possible so as to (1) conceal the fact that the idea is vague, or (2) elicit as broad or multivalent a response as possible. On the other hand, the librarian may be purposely ambiguous in order to (1) concede an inability to respond to the query, (2) buy time while considering possible responses, or (3) place the onus once again on the user to provide some clarity.

This interpersonal communication is of a largely subjective nature, as is virtually all of human behavior. Part of the subjectiveness is variously due to insufficient information (in which case the mind compensates by creating or assuming acceptable structures for the existing and missing information) or to an overabundance of information (in which case the mind is selective in what it uses to interpret a given body of data). In the former instance a person employs schemas to cope with certain situations. Schemas, as Jeremy Campbell notes,

> are structures of connected knowledge, acquired through our special experiences of being in the world, which are used to make sense of information that may be seriously deficient, strange, fragmentary, ambiguous, contradictory, or full of holes. They provide plausible scenarios, into which bits and pieces of data can be made to fit.[2]

These schemas are not solely, or even primarily, based on logic as part of the interpretive mechanism, but provide more of an analogic context in which to place the events experienced by the individual. In this way the human mind is better equipped to deal with the phenomena of the world, since the operative schema's analogs are built upon existing knowledge structures and formal logic is so general that it transcends the experiential world.

In the case of overabundant information, both verbal and nonverbal messages are being sent at a rate that may exceed a person's ability to assimilate and to infer meaning. Because of this a person makes choices, some of which may be arbitrary, as to what to receive. Behavior is then based on the responses to those messages received and interpreted. Lee Thayer writes,

> Each [individual] processes what each perceives to be the pertinent data in the situation, the consequence of which is some decision or thought, which in turn is immediate occasion for his behavior. . . . The behavior of one individual thus becomes *potential* data for the other, and so on. But each remains ultimately subjective; each functions consistently with his own psychological system. . . . "Communication" occurs when either person inputs data from his environment and converts the resulting raw sensory experiences into information to be utilized in thought or action—according to the ways in which he is uniquely programmed to do so.[3]

Although the concepts of Campbell and Thayer are not the same there is a consistent thread that runs through the passages. That thread may be seen as either a prevailing knowledge structure or an existing psychological state. Both concepts are part of a complex cognitive system that allows people to process the messages that bombard them. This system allows a person to walk in a city and, at one time, be oblivious to buildings, storefronts, and passing cars and people, and, at another time, be acutely aware of a particular message—a person, something in a store window. A library user employs this system when speaking with a librarian. The system attunes the person to certain messages that may be relevant to his or her need while other messages go unprocessed. Dysfunction may occur when the user's system focuses on a state, such as apprehension about approaching a librarian or fear that the request will not be expressed "properly," that is not conducive to reception of the messages intended to address the request.

The dysfunction just described is largely one of perception and perspective. Most reference librarians have worked with users who believe that their requests are stupid or that they are wasting the librarian's time. This springs from an all-too-popular perception that a library is a simple entity and that a person is somehow deficient if he or she cannot maneuver flawlessly through its retrieval and storage mechanisms. Unfortunately, some librarians are guilty of perpetuating the myth of simplicity. The danger of the myth is that it creates in the user a perspective of competence (or incompetence). That perspective will govern the user's cognitive system and will affect the success of the transaction. Librarians need to be aware of the power of the prevailing perspective. Let us first investigate how the players fit into some existing models.

THE LIBRARIAN IN COMMUNICATION MODELS

The role of the librarian in the simplest of communication models is much akin to that of the library. The major difference between library and librarian is the much greater possibility of feedback to work with the latter. Discussion here is now out of the realm of mass media; the source and receiver are in closer contact, which facilitates role reversal. The library user usually initiates the process by asking a question of the librarian. In the most rudimentary exchange there may be direct application of the linear model. A user may ask, "Where are the current magazines?" and the librarian could respond simply, "Third floor." No ambiguity is assumed, at least from the verbal cues provided by the user. Nonverbal cues may suggest to the librarian that another question is waiting to be asked. Stuart Glogoff addresses this issue and stresses the importance of the study of kinesis, or body language, to communication.[4] The emphasis here is on the verbal component of the process.

With a more complex query there is likely to be some degree of role reversal. The librarian, initially the receiver, becomes the source as reciprocal questioning becomes necessary. Each message sent provides feedback that influences the response. As David Berlo says, "Feedback provides the source with information concerning his success in accomplishing his objective. In doing this, it exerts control over future messages which the source encodes."[5] The feedback is effective if there is fidelity of the transmission of the message. A speech or hearing disorder, for instance, could result in failure of the process. Language difficulties could also wreak havoc with communication. If these difficulties are detected early on, there may be some compensation for them and a chance for success. This is especially so if the problem can be averted before confusion or frustration have an opportunity to set in.

The library literature includes some attempts at modeling the process of communication as it is manifest in reference transactions. One of the first and the simplest graphic representations of user–librarian communication was posited by Bernard Vavrek in 1974. His model presents a simple conceptual design based on a library patron (the source of inquiry), the reference librarian (the receiver of the message), and an inquiry. This design is a fundamental, unidirectional, linear representation, based on the kinds of queries usually initiated at a reference desk.[6] Vavrek's formulation, however, need not be limited to a single department in a library; its applicability can extend wherever the library user comes into contact with a librarian.

The assumption of Vavrek's model, though, is simplicity of the process itself. A straightforward inquiry is made of the librarian. The model may actually be more fittingly applied to user–library communication, since in that environment feedback is at best delayed. Feedback is missing from Vavrek's conceptualization, but is almost inevitable in a dyadic exchange. It would be simple to add feedback to the model, but it would still be a limited expression of what takes place in user–librarian communication. This inadequacy has been recognized in the literature and James Rettig has sought to create a more complex representation (see Figure 5.1).[7]

Integral to Rettig's model is the presence of feedback—actually a dual feedback mechanism aimed at reducing ambiguity at both the question and response stages. Within the concept of the model, feedback appears to be a fairly simple and straightforward thing. This is an not to imply that the model represents a deterministic system, as a true linear process might be. Rettig's representation, however, suggests that clarity can be arrived at through a sequence of directed and redirected questions, first by the librarian regarding the user's initial query and then regarding the potential outcome. There is an almost ontological assumption at work; there is, in the user's mind, a true question that is completely understood and there is also a true answer to the question. This is frequently not the case. In many such transactions the library user is essentially attempting to express what he or she does *not* know. It is, of course, difficult for a person to relate what is not known. The feedback mechanism depends on fidelity, just as is true of a technical communication system. Given that, does the response, "I don't know," constitute feedback? It is probably useful only in that it effectively eliminates one tack for questioning. Nonetheless, feedback is necessary and invaluable to sucess in librarian–user communication.

Watzlawick, Beavin, and Jackson articulate the importance of feedback as an event and as an idea in human communication.

Figure 5.1
Rettig Model

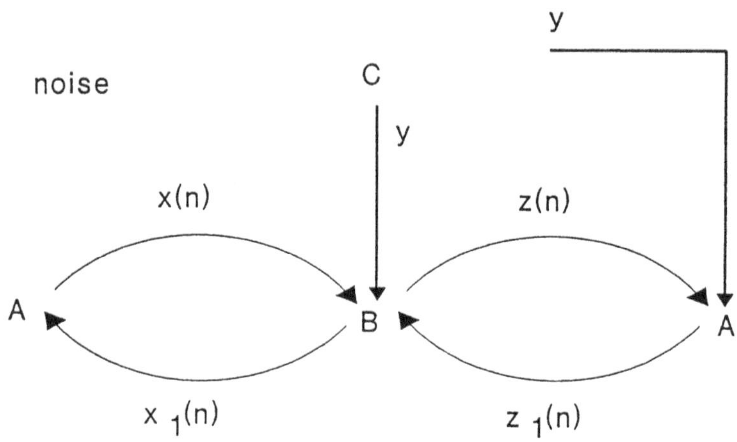

Key:

A an inquirer

B a librarian

C a mass medium information source

x an inquiry

x_1 feedback to an inquiry

y a message received from a mass medium information source

z a message sent by a librarian including information about and/or from a mass medium information source

z_1 feedback to a message z

n a variable number

Source: Reprinted with permission of the American Library Association, from *RQ*, Vol. 18 (Fall 1978), "*A Theoretical Model and Definition of the Reference Process*," by James Rettig, illustration on p. 23, © ALA.

While in linear, progressive chains of causality it is meaningful to speak about the beginning and end of a chain, these terms are meaningless in systems with feedback loops. There is no beginning and no end to a circle. Thinking in terms of such systems forces one to abandon the notion that, say, event *a* comes first and event *b* is determined by *a*'s occurrence, for by the same faulty logic it could be claimed that event *b* precedes *a*, depending on where one arbitrarily chooses to break the continuity of the circle.[8]

In the instance at hand, though, there is a beginning to the process and also an end (or at least a termination of the transaction). It would be impossible to analyze the phenomena if we believed it were circular. Circularity leads to the belief that there is no progress and no possible resolution. A more accurate and useful postulate is that the communication process is helical, as Frank Dance suggests. A helix includes a reflexive nature, but also signifies moving forward. If a librarian and a library user hope for a productive exchange, there has to be some progressive movement toward an answer to the query or a satisfaction of the need.

Norbert Wiener states that "feedback is a method of controlling a system by reinserting into it the results of past performance. . . . If . . . the information which proceeds backward from the performance is able to change the general method and pattern of performance, we have a process which may well be called learning."[9] The questioning process in a librarian–user exchange is meant to be cumulative, with each phase informing later phases. In this way there is a degree of control from the past. In this way, also, it constitutes a learning process as the initial query is answered and the conditions of that query are divulged (including incorporating feedback). The library user, in many cases, undergoes learning via communication by discovering aspects of the need or question not known or anticipated at the outset of the transaction. The initial query may have been incompletely formulated; the process fosters enhancement of clarity as contingencies are presented and alternatives explored. Through the endeavor the librarian may also learn about the mechanism of query response from the standpoint of technical facets (media to exploit) and communication (employing the Force of Clarity).

As Wiener also points out, feedback helps to reduce entropy. The purpose of the follow-up questioning is to bring some order to the situation. In Shannon and Weaver terms, this serves to reduce choice, to reduce the number of possible options for response. Unlike their application to technical communication systems, though, the process is not necessarily binary. Follow-up questions frequently do not offer choices of yes or no, zero or one. They do help to make some responses more likely by narrowing scope, breadth, and depth. The dilemma that still exists is the ontological problem. Entropy will be reduced if, initially, the library user's query has at least some degree of order. If it is disordered, the chance of the process imposing order is considerably reduced. The problem is akin to that of Clever Hans, a horse owned by Wilhelm von Osten shortly after the turn of this century. Hans was able to answer questions, some quite complex, by tapping his hoof. The correctness of his answer, however, depended on the inquisitor's knowledge of the answer, since Hans took his cues from the questioner's body language, which tended to betray correct answers.[10] In the library situation, if neither user nor librarian can recognize the appropriate response, disorder will probably remain high.

In existing general communication models the potential for feedback (directly or indirectly) and for other mechanisms aimed at enhancing success is noted. For instance, in Schramm's model the fields of experience suggest certain territories where communication can be facilitated. The model itself illustrates only one point in time; implied by it is some sort of feedback activity in order to define and map out the fields. Once determined, the overlap, or possible overlap, portends certain things for message construction.

- The message must be so designed and delivered as to gain the attention of the intended destination (receiver).
- The message must employ signs that refer to experience common to source and destination, so as to get the meaning across.
- The message must arouse personality needs in the destination and suggest some ways to meet those needs.
- The message must suggest a way to meet those needs that is appropriate to the group situation of the destination at the time when that person moved to make the desired response.[11]

It is important in considering the message to remember the context of the transaction and the relationship, usually formal and somewhat prescribed, between the librarian and the user. The context of structured inquiry and response will determine, to a considerable extent, the discovery of common fields of experience and so, especially for the librarian, help define the kind and form of message created. In this way the librarian may know whether to take a technical or generalist approach, whether to provide detailed background or to move to the specific of the response.

Also of importance in considering the kind of communication represented by librarian–user exchanges is the state of the receiver of a message. As is discussed above, both the librarian and the user act as receivers at various times during the transaction and their behavior as receivers is influenced by a complex set of factors. For instance, Donald MacKay points out that the receiver in any communication process has a range of states of readiness. This means that a receiver's ability or willingness to accept communication varies. There may be physiological or psychological factors that affect the states of readiness, and the causes for variation may be external or internal. The range is not constant from day to day or even from transaction to transaction. The range may be quite narrow at some times and fairly broad at others. Message selection, that is, the possibility of interpretation of the message, can be made from any of those states within the range. "A meaningless message is one that makes no selection from the range. An ambiguous message is one that could make more than one selection."[12] The narrower the range, the better the chance that the intended selection lies outside the range. The scope of the range is affected by intellectual factors (the knowledge base of either the librarian or the user), cognitive factors (the ability to interpret the structure of the message), and psychological or emotional factors (which may be unrelated to the message or its sender).

Another aspect of the receiver, especially in a formal setting such as a library, is the effect of the organization and the organizational role of the librarian. This role determines, or helps determine, the range of states of readiness for the organizational participants. This determination can be overt in the form of rules or procedures; it is more likely to be a more subtle influence based on institutional purpose and expectations of members. Mickey Smith refers to this influence as "mission."

> Missions refer to what we are organized for—the purpose of our organization. We form a set of concepts, a set of rules about organization, each of us has a place in the organization and a function within it. This function is bound by the communication rules within the mission that are worked out for that mission only. . . . My contention here is that the mission itself is a separate functional area of communication, with mission-related information, and a separate set of rules governing the exchanges that differ from the rules in any other functional area. Mission-based communication contains memory (the past), cognitive and emotional information and something else too—the structure of the mission itself.[13]

The mission orientation helps to limit both the possibilities for the librarian and the expectations of the user. It serves almost as a pre-definition of the scope of potential queries that, while broad, sets some parameters for the exchange. It helps to establish a sort of playing field and dictates some basic rules for the game. This function may be seen as a means of controlling, or trying to control, entropy.

Of course, the librarian–user exchange need not be limited to a dyad. There is certainly no rule in libraries that only the librarian who is approached by the user may respond to the query. Drawing again from the thinking of Mickey Smith, it is logical and reasonable to expect the knowledge bases of two or more people to be more expansive than that of one person. There will, naturally, be some overlap (there would have to be for these individuals to be able to communicate at all), but each will have a unique span of knowledge. This is not, and is not meant to be, a revelation. Effective librarians do not hestiate to incorporate the knowledge of colleagues, of individuals affiliated with other agencies, or information available from remote sources. I realize the mention of "effective" librarianship is problematic. Some studies maintain that, where service fails, it is because there is a lack of referral to other departments of the library and to other entities outside the library.[14] Nonetheless, the broadening of the communication spectrum is important to the provision of an information-based service. See Chapter 4 (Figure 4.1) for an illustration of overlap and the potential for expansion beyond the resources of a single library. In communication terms, what is needed is a willingness to initiate a process beyond the constraints of the dyadic transaction.

Smith further notes that there are sets of protocols that govern the messages passing between people. At the most rudimentary levels are verbal protocols, the encoding and decoding of words—librarian and user must understand one another. Rachael Naismith and Joan Stein examined comprehension by users of some technical terms commonly used by librarians.[15] Many terms are misunderstood by users and the meaning of some technical terms is gleaned only through morphological analysis (breaking down a word to its separate structural parts, defining each part, and putting the definitions together in an interpretation) or multiword unpacking (a similar process of decomposition, but at the word level). This means that comprehension is likely to break down at the *word* level, not necessarily at some higher conceptual level. If the user is not able to understand a term or phrase employed by a librarian, the cognitive reaction may be to focus attention on that word or phrase. In concentrating effort on decoding the segment, the entire message may be lost. If the sticking point is central to the entire communication, then that communication is in jeopardy. In their work Naismith and Stein acknowledge the discourse model of communication articulated by Terry Winograd.[16] This model incorporates the existence and use of schemas (discussed in the previous chapter). The model is sufficiently inclusive to take into account each individual's model or conception of the other, so that social conventions, relational roles, and linguistic interpretation might be components of the process. These expectations help define the context of the construction and interpretation of the message.

It is possible, then, that a breakdown of verbal protocols could result in encoding or decoding errors. In fact, not only is it possible, but Naismith and Stein show that it is all too probable. In approaching a remedy they write,

> Given that patrons only understand 50 percent of what librarians say or write, what are the options available to library staff members for closing this gap? The following represents a list of options ranging from the least to most accommodating:
>
> - use terms without defining them, and let the patron sink or swim
> - use terms without defining them but be alert to verbal and nonverbal cues from the patron indicating confusion
> - solicit feedback from the user as you go along, asking, for instance, "Interlibrary loan—do you know what that is?"
> - use visual aids to assist the patron, such as pointing to the components of a citation
> - define terms the first time they are used in an interaction or publication, then use them subsequently within definition
> - use formal library instruction to teach library technical language
> - append glossaries of terms to written publications
> - avoid local terms not useful for patrons' future needs
> - define technical terms whenever you use them
> - avoid jargon altogether[17]

Some combination of the intermediating suggestions is likely to be most effective for the user and most efficient for the librarian. Different situations will require varying solutions and different modes of learning may necessitate a flexible approach.

Not surprisingly, the examination of Naismith and Stein is consistent with other, more general, studies of word comprehension and the phenomenon of lexical interpretation. Sharon Mutter and Shahin Hashtroudi conducted some experiments dealing with the effects of word frequency. In general they found that unfamiliar, low frequency words require greater cognitive effort and more extensive processing than do familiar, high frequency words.[18] Considering these two studies together suggests some strategies for librarian–user communication. It may be necessary for a librarian to define certain terms in the course of communication. Beyond that, some extra time may be required for the user to process these terms and their definitions since, at the most basic level, the user is effectively expanding his or her lexicon. That effort may pay off in the long term, especially if the user is going to be a frequent user, but in the short term there are costs to the communication process—either in time expended on understanding or in confusion or misunderstanding.

The problems discussed above are, for the most part, semantic. I mean this in the technical, linguistic, sense rather than as the word has crept into popular usage. Semantics, as a branch of linguistics, is concerned primarily with meaning and the difficulties noted stem from obstacles to the inference of meaning. As F. R. Palmer observes, semantics is problematic because "meanings do not seem to be stable but to depend upon speakers, hearers and context."[19] Problems of communication in a library frequently cannot be isolated to a single, identifiable, cause. In fact, some individuals believe that isolation may not be possible at all. For instance, Ray Jackendoff takes the approach that meaning in language and the nature of perception and cognition are inseparable.[20] Similarly, Smith incorporates into his communication model cognitive protocols as well as verbal ones. This involves the encoding and decoding of concepts and transcends the word level of understanding. For optimum communication in a librarian–user exchange, attention must be paid to the cognitive protocols. Being able to understand the words "call number" will help the library user locate a particular item in a library. Being able to understand the concept of classification will assist that user in making connections among containers of like content.

Realization of the working of a cognitive aspect (and its functioning along with a linguistic aspect) are implicit, though not necessarily explicit, in other communication models. Barnlund's model is an example of the subtle, less overt, implications of cognitive activity. This model incorporates a wider range of behavioral cues (just the use of the word "behavioral" connotes something that is not static, that is dynamic and changing), including nonverbal cues. Such cues are not relegated to a single dimension of meaning, but incorporate a deeper perceptual phenomenon. Further, Barnlund recognizes the existence of private cues, a cognitive process of integrating the various cues, internal and external, to the dyad. The garbage can model is also one implying a decision process that necessitates the connection of disparate semantic cues. This may include selection among conflicting messages and interpretations, depicting clearly the cognitive imperative inherent in complex communication.

THE LIBRARIAN AS CHANNEL

In the preceding chapter the role of the library as channel was explored. Such a role probably makes intuitive sense because there is a general acceptance of the library as a mechanism for mediation between the user and information. The librarian, too, is spoken of as an intermediary, but the librarian's functioning as channel is not quite as obvious as the library's. What the librarian does is sometimes perceived as a gatekeeper role. The gatekeeper, according to Werner Severin and James Tankard, is one who "determines what information is passed along the chain and how faithfully it is reproduced."[21] This is, by its very nature, a selective activity—it must be or the library user would be inundated by information. John Bittner expands the notion of gatekeeper a bit and allows for a gatekeeper group, which might be one view of librarianship as a whole.[22] He also conceives of a gatekeeper chain, a structure of levels regulating the flow of information. This latter mechanism could be translated into the collection development activity in a library, which determines the specific physical items to be acquired, and reference activity, which is, to an extent, defined by what items are collected. Since the process is selective, the gatekeeper is influenced by a number of forces, some of which are conscious. Bittner recognizes some of these factors affecting choice as economics, legal restrictions, the presence of deadlines, ethics, competition, attention factors, peer pressure, and the reaction to feedback.[23]

Traditional reference services may be the clearest embodiment of the function of gatekeeper, which is essentially that of channel (but with a conscious, selective, element thrown in so that the librarian is simultaneously source and channel in a kind of subset of the larger communication perspective). Elsewhere I have written that

> the library provides access to more information than any individual user needs or wants at any given time. It may even have more information on a particular, relatively narrow, subject than the user needs or wants. One or more communication exchanges, each of which can be represented by the [linear] communication model (or by Rettig's model, which includes feedback and a circular structure), are engaged in by the user and the librarian to determine how much and what kind of information is required. Other exchanges are then made to get the information to the user. In this way communication may be seen as a combination of macro and microprocesses. . . . The macroprocess is the very basic one of a user receiving information. It, however, is dependent upon the microprocesses; the breakdown of any microprocess could well mean the failure of the entire communication process. In this way the centrality of the role of the librarian (and the risk inherent in the process) becomes evident. The concept of freedom of choice written of by Weaver also becomes evident (although here information is more closely tied to meaning). The macroprocess, with its component microprocesses, constitutes a means of limiting choice to the (likely) more relevant items. The purpose of this is to render communication less random and to impose the structure of meaning on it.[24]

It may be more useful to envision the librarian as being a subset of the channel or, and this may be the most accurate depiction, a channel facilitator. The librarian may function in a way similar to a combination tuner and amplifier. It is the librarian's job, first of all, to focus and define. This involves attempting to glean the actual query imbedded in the stated query and then making the connection between that and the body of information available. This available information takes a variety of forms, each of which offers unique constraints and opportunities. It would be useful to look more closely at the nature of these forms, and John Murdock and David Liston have provided a description of channels that can be incorporated here.

The Direct Channel. One extreme of the communication continuum (included in the direct, nonrecorded transfer channel of the model) is face-to-face discussion in which communication is:

1. Very direct.
2. Very dynamic, permitting the utilization of:
   - words, phrases, sentences, etc. (language);
   - gesticulations;
   - inflections in the voice;
   - interruptability, allowing the receiver to interrupt the sender requesting clarification of or elaboration on the message being spoken;
   - feedback, allowing the receiver to become the sender with reverse flow of information transfer.
3. Very rapid, with virtually no delay time involved.

   Disadvantages primarily relate to:

   1. faulty memory;
   2. little chance for study of what is transferred;
   3. frequent acceptability of vague generalizations that would not be permitted in a recorded message.

The Primary Recorded Media Channel. Eventually the point is reached where the originator feels that what he has to say should be recorded as part of the body of literature of his discipline. This publication is usually thought of as the primary literature dealing with current topics. . . . Other examples of primary recorded media are letters, newspapers, conference notes, technical reports, handbooks, monographs, texts, patents, and tapes.

The Archival Channel. Because the user is not always sensitized to the flow of messages through the more current channels, the archival channel has developed to store information for subsequent delayed usage when the user becomes aware of a need for it.

The Secondary Recorded Media Channel. The next channel for the transfer of information involves the secondary sources or media. It feeds from both the primary recorded media and archives and also becomes archival when collected into libraries and other holdings. The purpose of the secondary recorded media channel is to assist people to search more easily through an ever-increasing volume of current and stored information for items of interest.

The Information Center Channel. This channel represents an attempt to provide a service to essentially a known group of users upon demand. . . . Thinking in terms of an electrical analogy to the model, information centers act as "switching centers," utilizing the "circuitry" of the channels in the most appropriate combination of series and parallel arrangements.[25]

It is not difficult to see that the librarian not infrequently acts as a direct channel. Essentially the librarian explores his or her own mind as an information storage and retrieval mechanism. A database of information and knowledge exists that can be tapped when appropriate. With the other manifestations of channel, all of which are relevant to the library, the librarian is more of a channel facilitator. The user may well require assistance dealing with recorded media and the intricacies of storing them. For instance, the media have to be organized for access, and the organization is not always self-evident.

This analysis is more complex because the observer and the observed are autonomous. This is especially difficult with communication because it is unavoidable. Klaus Krippendorff writes,

The crucial difference between studying a system from the outside or from the within lies in the properties of the observers. In systems involving their observers, the properties of its observers enter the system under consideration, often as constitutive components, and a theory of communication in such systems must account for this.[26]

This notion recognizes the fallacy of positivism in any research endeavor focusing on human behavior. The fallacy, however, is a clinging one, as Michael Harris notes.[27] It endures primarily because of its attractiveness to a field that yearns for an ontological assurance of a sometimes primitive empiricism. As Krippendorff further states, though, "Ontological commitments simply rule that the observers' properties may not enter their domain of observation and, to retain this commitment, efforts must be directed to minimize their effects. Ontological commitments therefore become untenable in the study of communication in systems involving their observers."[28]

Borrowing properties from components can be extended to the system itself. All participants in the library, even indirect ones such as authors, publishers, and producers, become part of the system, thus bringing their own ideals, values, goals, and purposes to the communication structure. This goes for the channels and media also. The library is influenced by the properties of the channels and media it chooses to include and employ. This harkens back to Marshall McLuhan. The library's physical arrangement is based on the kinds of artifacts and technology it houses or provides access to. Any librarian can attest that those influences are not static. Further, the library is influenced by the uses to which it is put. The activity at all levels, including intra- and extra-organizational, dictates hierarchy and relationships, which can define communication. The librarian is also subject to all these influences and incorporates them into individual behavior. The effect may manifest itself as an emphasis on visual, rather than verbal, presentation or as a reliance on nonbook materials. In the communication process the languages of the media may be adopted in order to deal with, say, videos or compact discs. The question relevant here is: Are these languages any more intelligible to users than is the language of libraries? To those who have been introduced to the media in other contexts, the answer is likely to be yes. To others, the answer would be no. Effectively there may be a trade of one set of jargon for another.

Of course the message may be altered by its passage through a channel. George Miller addresses this issue in generic terms.

If you put a message in at one end of the channel, another message comes out the other end. So the communication engineer talks about the "input" to the channel and "output" from the channel. For a good channel, the input and the output are closely related but usually not identical. The input is changed, more or less, in the process of transmission. If the changes are random, the communication engineer talks about "noise" in the channel. Thus the output depends upon both the input and the noise.[29]

We cannot ignore that, just as the librarian can be envisioned as a channel facilitator, so too can the librarian's mind and facility with language be seen as facilitators for the librarian. The mind, in this respect, is functioning as an instrument of interpretation; it connects information at hand with stored information to make decisions about relevance and inclusiveness. That interpretation must then be expressed in some way, and language is that way. These steps involve some alteration that may or may not result in a loss of fidelity. The librarian needs to be aware of the intracacies of the process in order to use it to its optimum efficacy.

THE CONVERGENCE MODEL

The linear communication model has been used as a jumping-off point for discussion. This has been helpful because it establishes roles and elements of the process and defines these components clearly. The linear model is not sufficient, though, primarily because of its unidirectional nature, but also because of its mechanistic assumptions. Considering it was developed to describe technical communication, this is not necessarily a flaw in the model. Applications of the model, however, have frequently taken insufficient notice of its original purpose and have tried to extend it beyond its limits. Even the addition of feedback as a concept and as a mechanism has not resulted in an accurate depiction of what goes on in communication. Feedback, as applied in many models, is still a linear function. It is behavioristic in nature; it is similar to a description of stimulus and response. The limitations probably become evident with consideration of the points made in these chapters. Library/librarian–user communication is a complex phenomenon, with many possible motivations and many possible manifestations. The structure of the library and librarian–user exchanges virtually guarantees that the process cannot be linear.

At this point I think it is important to add one more communication model to the repertoire. Everett Rogers and Lawrence Kincaid have developed a model that is based on their perceived shortcomings of thinking about communication.

> The main problem with the linear models of communication stemmed from their basic metatheoretical or epistemological assumptions about the nature of information, how it is transmitted, and what we do with it. . . . These assumptions (1) that information is only a physical substance and (2) that individual minds are separate, led to seven biases that we identify in past communication theory and research.
>
> 1. A view of communication as a linear, one-way act (usually vertical), rather than a cyclical, two-way process over time.
> 2. A source bias based on dependency, rather than focusing on the relationship of those who communicate and their fundamental interdependency.
> 3. A tendency to focus on the objects of communication as simple, isolated physical objects, at the expense of the context in which they exist.
> 4. A tendency to focus on the messages per se at the expense of silence, and the punctuation and timing of messages.
> 5. A tendency to consider the primary function of communication to be persuasion, rather than mutual understanding, consensus, and collective action.
> 6. A tendency to concentrate on the psychological effects of communication on separate individuals, rather than on the social effects and the relationships among individuals within networks.
> 7. A belief in one-way mechanistic causation, rather than mutual causation, which characterizes human information systems that are fundamentally cybernetic.[30]

More specifically, they recognize the limitations of feedback as it has been incorporated into models and theories.

> The feedback loop, which improved the S-M-C-R [Source-Message-Channel-Receiver] model, is insufficient because it only carried (by definition) knowledge of the effects back to the source for his/her evaluation. This linear model excluded the effects of the source's messages on the source, an effect which may often be greater than the effect on the "receiver." Also excluded were the social effects of communication on other individuals who at the time are not considered the primary receivers of the source's message, even though these social effects sometimes are greater than the immediate effects on the primary receiver. Realization of such indirect effects gave rise to the two-step flow and multistep flow hypotheses in mass communication research; they deal with the relay of the source's original message to second, third, fourth, and other levels of "receivers." Communication research focused on the source's message to the initial receiver, although the recognition of multistepped flows suggested the greater complexity of the human communication process.[31]

We may be tempted to think that when a librarian–user exchange is terminated, the process ends. The user, though, may carry the information obtained to others outside the library. They may alter their behavior in some ways on the basis of the information. At the other end, the librarian may communicate with colleagues about the transaction. Information resulting from the exchange may become part of an extended body of knowledge relevant to a reference department, for instance. The transaction may also prompt changes in policy if unforeseen difficulties arise in the course of the transaction. This is a rather simplistic example of the ideas put forth by Rogers and Kincaid.

Rogers and Kincaid base their model, which they call a "convergence model," on the sign theory of C. S. Peirce. They recognize that

> Every symbol, word, sentence, or scientific formula must be given meaning if it is to communicate intelligent thought. . . . The meaning of

any utterance is revealed by the reply that it evokes, which in turn needs a return reply to interpret it, and so on, in a potentially endless sequence. Recognition of this sequential aspect of communication means that the competent use of understanding of any sign is always a matter of degree. Peirce's insights capture the two basic principles underlying the convergence model: that information is inherently imprecise and uncertain, and that communication is a dynamic process of development over time.[32]

The result is the graphic model in Figure 5.2.[33]

Of course, the model assumes an ideal—the reaching of mutual understanding. Inherent in the model, though, are implications for dysfunction. Communication, being a dynamic process, is dependent on the continual alteration, confirmation, or edification of the component parts depicted in the model. The extent to which these checks and balances are possible in the kind of communication discussed here is a function of the finality of each exchange. A particular exchange may be terminated by more or less mutual consent, even when there has not been any mutual understanding. The complexity of the process is such, however, that neither participant is aware of the lack of understanding, at least at that moment. There is usually a formality to the exchanges and other constraints, such as available time, which makes the creation and sharing of a sufficient amount and quality of information difficult. When the constraints are less evident, the potential for the attainment of mutual understanding is greater. Success is dependent on a lessening of the constraints, so that the necessary exploration of each participant understanding and modification of the information and its presentation can occur.

There is one important and frequently-occurring constraint that is missing from their model: the effects of external influences on these components. Interference from the influences is usually referred to as noise. That phenomenon is the topic of the next chapter.

Figure 5.2
Rogers/Kincaid Model

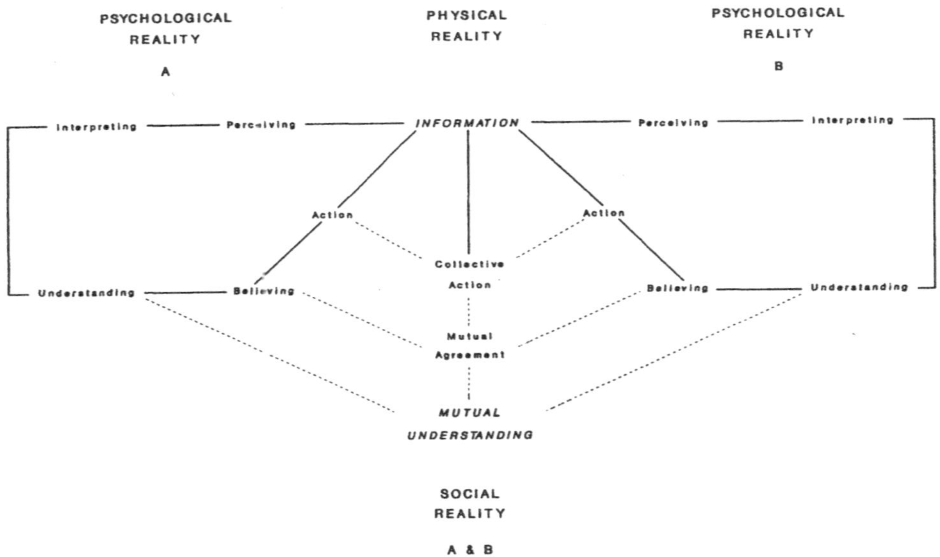

Source: Reprinted with permission of The Free Press, a Division of Macmillan, Inc. from *Communication Networks: Toward a New Paradigm for Research* by Everett M. Rogers and D. Lawrence Kincaid. Copyright © 1981 by The Free Press.

NOTES

1. Marilyn Merritt, "On Questions Following Questions in Service Encounters," *Language in Society*, 5 (December 1976), 316–17.

2. Jeremy Campbell, *The Improbable Machine* (New York: Simon & Schuster, 1989), 92.

3. Lee Thayer, "Communication and Organization Theory," in *Human Communication Theory: Original Essays*, ed. Frank E. X. Dance (New York: Holt, Rinehart and Winston, 1967), 91.

4. Stuart Glogoff, "Communication Theory's Role in the Reference Interview," *Drexel Library Quarterly*, 19 (Spring 1983), 56–72.

5. David Berlo, *The Process of Communication* (New York: Holt, Rinehart, and Winston, 1960), 111–12.

6. Bernard Vavrek, "The Nature of Reference Librarianship," *RQ*, 13 (Spring 1974), 214.

7. James Rettig, "A Theoretical Model and Definition of the Reference Process," *RQ*, 18 (Fall 1978), 23.

8. Paul Watzlawick, Janet Helmick Beavin, and Don D. Jackson, *Pragmatics of Human Communication* (New York: W. W. Norton & Co., 1967), 46.

9. Norbert Wiener, *The Human Use of Human Beings: Cybernetics and Society* (New York: Houghton Mifflin, 1954), 68.

10. Paul Watzlawick, *How Real is Real: Communication, Disinformation, Confusion* (London: Souvenir, 1983), 30–33.

11. Wilbur Schramm, "How Communication Works," in *Mass Communication: Selected Readings for Librarians*, ed. K. J. McGarry (Hamden, CT: Linnet Books and Clive Bingley, 1972), 26.

12. Donald M. MacKay, *Information, Mechanism, and Meaning* (Cambridge, Massachusetts Institute of Technology Press, 24.

13. Mickey Smith, "A Model of Human Communication," *IEEE Communications Magazine*, 26 (February 1988), 5–6.

14. See, for instance, the studies reported in Peter Hernon and Charles R. McClure, *Unobtrusive Testing and Library Reference Services* (Norwood, NJ: Ablex, 1987).

15. Rachael Naismith and Joan Stein, "Library Jargon: Student Comprehension of Technical Language Used by Librarians," *College & Research Libraries*, 50 (September 1989), 543–52.

16. Terry Winograd, "A Framework for Understanding Discourse," in *Cognitive Processes in Comprehension*, ed. Marcel Adam Just and Patricia A. Carpenter (Hillsdale, NJ: Lawrence Erlbaum Assoc., Pubs., 1977), 67.

17. Naismith and Stein, "Library Jargon," 551.

18. Sharon A. Mutter and Shahin Hashtroudi, "Cognitive Effort and the Word Frequency Effect in Recognition and Lexical Decision," *American Journal of Psychology*, 100 (Spring 1987), 113.
19. F. R. Palmer, *Semantics*, 2d ed. (Cambridge: Cambridge University Press, 1981), 7.
20. Ray Jackendoff, *Semantics and Cognition* (Cambridge: Massachusetts Institute of Technology Press, 1983), 19–22.
21. Werner J. Severin and James W. Tankard, Jr., *Communication Theories* (New York: Hastings House, 1979), 48.
22. John R. Bittner, *Foundations of Communication* (Englewood Cliffs, NJ: Prentice-Hall, 1985), 375.
23. Ibid., 377–80.
24. John Budd, "The User and the Library: A Discussion of Communication," *The Reference Librarian*, No. 20 (1987), 215–16.
25. John W. Murdock and David M. Liston, Jr., "A General Model of Information Transfer: Theme Paper 1968 Annual Convention," *American Documentation*, 18 (October 1967), 198–200.
26. Klaus Krippendorff, "An Epistemological Foundation for Communication," *Journal of Communication*, 34 (Summer 1984), 31.
27. Michael H. Harris, "The Dialectic of Defeat: Antinomies [sic] in Research in Library and Information Science," *Library Trends*, 34 (Spring 1986), 515–31.
28. Krippendorff, "An Epistemological Foundation," 31.
29. George A. Miller, "What Is Information Measurement?" *American Psychologist*, 8 (January 1953), 6.
30. Everett M. Rogers and D. Lawrence Kincaid, *Communication Networks: Toward a New Paradigm for Research* (New York: Free Press, 1981), 38–39.
31. Ibid., 70.
32. Ibid., 44.
33. Ibid., 55.

6

Noise

Strongest minds
Are often those of whom the noisy world
Hears least

William Wordsworth, "The Excursion"

KINDS OF NOISE

The primary focus of this book is on communication in libraries, but the implication of communication and its importance reaches beyond an organization—even one that may be seen as a social institution, a social good. We are products of our past. Everything that has gone before has served as the infrastructure of the society we now live in. The past has helped to construct our intellectual foundation, our legal underpinnings, our societal lineaments. Realization of this aided Jesse Shera in formulating his diagram of culture (see Figure 6.1).[1]

The importance of communication to Shera is obvious in the diagram. Its centrality is essential because "culture is impossible without some medium for the transmission of thought. Human thought is social as well as personal, and communication binds the

Figure 6.1
Shera's Diagram of Culture

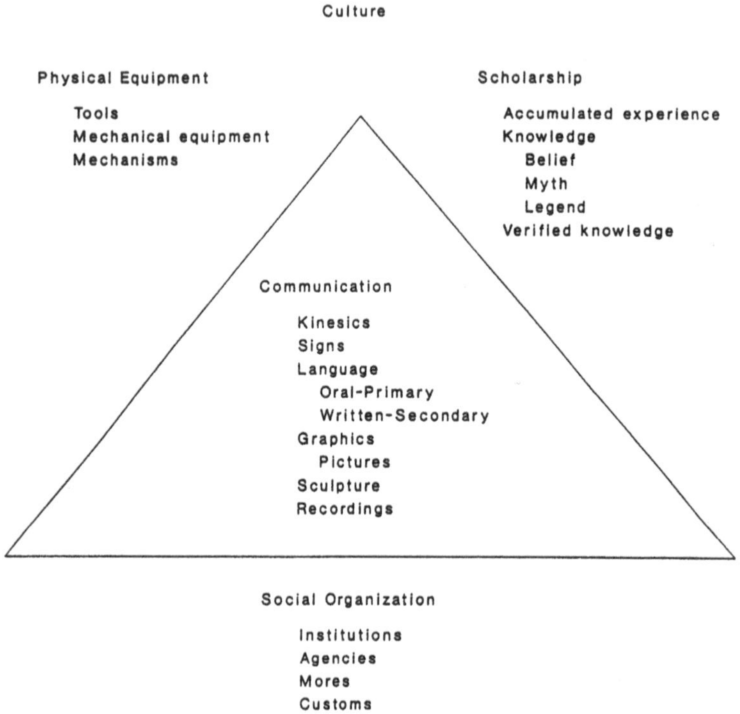

Source: Jesse H. Shera, *Introduction to Library Science: Basic Elements of Library Service* (Littleton, CO: Libraries Unlimited, 1976), 44. Copyright 1976, Libraries Unlimited, Inc., P.O. Box 3988, Englewood, CO 80155-3988. Reprinted with permission of the publisher.

culture into a cohesive whole and makes possible the control which it exerts within society."[2]

Shera further observes,

> Social epistemology, as I envisage it, is fundamental to the librarian because it should provide an effective philosophical frame of reference within which can be viewed and understood the complexities of the

intellectual processes of society—an understanding of how society as a whole seeks to achieve a perception of its *total* [emphasis Shera's] intellectual and social environment.[3]

This involves the transmission of human thought, the communication of those intellectual processes. Of course, this means that people have to employ some media in order to communicate thought; language is such a medium. It might be inferred that segments of this book argue that language has what Noam Chomsky refers to as an "essential purpose." Chomsky eschews this notion, stating that such a limitation ignores the various functions of language or assumes a definition of communication that is too broad to be useful.[4] Communication, then, is *one* purpose of language, and one that is central here.

Communication is not only a complex process, then, but one with a relatively low probability for success. Problems both internal and external to the individual and to the system—the dyad or the group, for example—impinge upon the chances for communication to occur. Pondering this could lead to some assessment of the phenomenological essence, the eidos, of communication, but at this point the prospect of communication will be examined in a bit more mundane fashion. We can label that generic deterrent to communication "noise." There are some kinds or classifications of noise that can be examined, especially in the library setting; these kinds first need to be described. Once described, we can use the heightened awareness to control for, combat, or at the very least recognize the potential forces affecting communication.

For purposes of discussion we will divide noise into four types. The first we can label "literal" noise—audible interference that comes between the source and the receiver. This kind of noise is one of the most prevalent difficulties afflicting technical communication, and the simplest to understand and eliminate. A second kind of noise may be called "linguistic" noise. This may manifest itself as a lack of sharing language or problems affecting the inference of meaning. This was covered at some length earlier; as was stated, the difficulty centers around *shared* language and that language may, on the face of it, appear to be shared when in actuality it is not. The third type is "internal" noise. While related to linguistic noise, this deals more with symbolic meaning and the interpretation of messages that have been received. The fourth category can be classed as "psychological" noise. Overload is one way this occurs. Overload may be considered a variety of literal noise, but it is not precisely an interference between source and receiver; rather, it is a phenomenon that affects the selection of messages relevant to a given context. Each of these types will be examined more closely.

LITERAL NOISE

In technical communication, such as telephone, radio, or television transmission, there is always the possibility of some interference due to weather, other natural occurrences, or some technical disorder. This kind of noise may or may not interfere with the reception and understanding of a message. Fred Dretske points out that the same amount of noise in separate instances could have different effects. He gives as examples two radio reports:

> (a) There will be rain on Sunday (snap, crackle, pop, hiss) has a good deal of noise, but the noise does not interfere with any part of the message being transmitted from the radio studio. . . . (b) There will be rain on (snap)-nday (crackle, pop, hiss). Here we have the same amount of noise, but the amount of transmitted information is reduced because the noise increases the equivocation. The equivocation is increased because part of the signal from the broadcasting studio is obscured, leaving an ambiguous (equivocal) message.[5]

Dretske's examples are the result of noise transmitted over the same channel as the message. In the model of communication by Shannon and Weaver presented earlier, the entrance of noise is clearly demonstrated as an intrusion into the channel and a disruption of the transmission of the message. In practical terms, this means that the message sent is not the same as the message received; it is altered by the noise to the point that the noise becomes part of the message. Naturally, the implied meaning of the sender may well be lost.

Noise is a deleterious intruder because it introduces entropy. Order in communication is difficult enough to create (introduce, impose); noise disrupts the order that exists and decreases the probability of meaning inference. Imagine conversing with a friend on a busy street at rush hour. Think about how many statements or questions have to be repeated because of car horns, sirens, shouts, and so on. In fact, noise can attack any of the senses and disrupt communication. Orrin Klapp recognizes the scope of possible noise and writes,

> noise might occur anywhere that information is communicated, such as radio static, computer garbage, headlight glare, specks that spoil a photographic negative, typographical errors, distortion of rumors, genetic noise, interference between brain hemispheres, and so on. In this broad sense, noise is a concept fundamental for analysis of all biological and social systems as well as of information technology—a communicational form of entropy, intruding into and degrading information, at the human level opposed to meaning by its randomness and lack of message.[6]

As Klapp notes, noise, when conceived on this scale, can be organic—that is, afflicting one organism, one person—or systemic, which is to say, pervasive enough to affect a group, a body, an entire society. Thus, noise may be much more than a minor irritant.

Klapp further observes a more subtle, but probably more pernicious and virulent, kind of noise—noise that tries to pass itself off as information or communication.

> It is an irony of the information society that information gets in its own way—or, as one might put it, communication becomes noise to its own signal. . . . Sheer loudness makes any signal noisy because, whether information or nonsense, its strength drowns out other stimuli that might be signals. . . . Irrelevance or disconnectedness makes it harder to find a

pattern. . . . When information is too disconnected, finding its meaning becomes like a gigantic, endless jigsaw puzzle of which the pieces do not fit. . . . Bad complexity contains maximum disorder, expressed by names like jumble, hodgepodge, clutter, tangle, snarl. . . . Stylistic noise comes not from mere change of styles but clash of incompatible values. . . . Stylistic noise always threatens some identity—presenting signals and models (noise) incompatible with the identity a person or group wishes to preserve. . . . Pseudo-information . . . purports to tell us something but in fact tells nothing. Names such as hype, hokum, rhetoric, B.S., ballyhoo, shuck, schmalze, fake factor, buildup, puffery, and image building warn us not to take at face value much of what we hear even though one cannot pin down exactly what is wrong with it.[7]

It is evident in the above listing by Klapp that the key to noise is the blockage of meaning inference. For this reason, a category such as "pseudo-information" can be included. Also for this reason, such phenomena as disinformation or misinformation may be included. As was noted in an earlier chapter, neither of these qualifies as information, since they in no way inform. They are, however, forms of communication; some message is sent over some channel to some receiver. The usual intent of disinformation is to deceive rather than to inform. It is likely that because of the intent behind disinformation—presumed to be action taken for a purpose aimed at the good of the group, frequently of the body politic—it is dignified with such a term, rather than being classified as a lie. There is a distinction to be made, though, between disinformation and other forms of literal noise: disinformation does not prevent, or even impede, meaning inference; it directs such activity to a desired end. With disinformation or deliberate misinformation noise does not enter the channel and interfere with the transmission of a message-bearing signal. It is initiated by the source, but with the purpose intended that the source's message will override any other messages. Disinformation is what Paul Watzlawick calls "noncontingent;" the message is not a logical extension of events or an accurate account of certain happenings.[8] Its outcome is much the same as other forms of noise—the receiver is not able to base inferences on reliable signals.

It is the intentional nature of disinformation, misinformation, and much pseudo-information that separates it from other noise. These and most other forms of noise are imposed from without, but some noise is self-imposed. Klapp states that we choose some of the noise that envelopes us.

> We note that our information society is also a high-noise society. We live in a perpetual din of media, which we continually adapt to. Multi-media people listen with all their senses, trying to stay abreast of all developments. It is not at all unusual to have the television or radio on while reading a newspaper, eating breakfast, and now and then talking to somebody. We may also carry a watch or pocket page whose beeping signals remind us to move along to new stimuli. We may also carry a cassette recorder ("ghetto blaster") as we walk down the street—adding noise for everyone else—or wear a "Walkman," giving continual entertainment in our own sonic cocoon.[9]

LINGUISTIC NOISE

In previous discussion some of the problems of a lack of shared language were mentioned. As was noted, the most obvious instance is when two people speak different languages with neither having an understanding of the other's language. The problem of national or regional differences also may lead to a lack of sharing. These difficulties are obvious and are dictated in part by geography and by custom. Time is also an element when we think of linguistic noise. How many people really understand the following:

> For 'tis sport to have the enginer
> Hoist with his own petar.
>
> *Hamlet*, Act III, scene 4

How many reading this passage now know that a petar was an explosive device? To how many of today's readers is Shakespeare noise? The same might apply to works written earlier in this century. As semantic fashions change, words or phrases that were easily understood at the time they were written may no longer be intelligible. The reason for the difficulty is not that the words are meaningless or even that meaning was not implied by the author; with time and changing patterns, though, the implication may be lost.

An underlying reason for the more subtle language problems we experience is that language is, in most ways, a social phenomenon. If human beings could have developed a different means of communication (and especially if that means were less equivocal than language), then language might never have developed. One of its primary purposes is to allow one person to make things known to another. The fact that there are problems or improbabilities is due to the complexities of the social networks that we, as humans, are part of. These networks may be large and may overlap, but they are finite; they have boundaries. Within each network are sets of norms, goals, and behaviors that help to define the network and that may assist in making any given network inclusive or exclusive. So, when any two individuals meet, they are able to communicate with varying levels of success, depending on how much is shared. R. A. Hudson recognizes the limitation:

> We can be sure that no two speakers have the same language, because no two speakers have the same experience of language. The differences between speakers may vary from the very slight and trivial (in the case of twins brought up together, for instance) to total difference within whatever limits are set by universal characteristics of language. . . . The individual speaker is presumably molded much more by experience (as a listener) than by his genetic make-up, and his experience consists in fact of speech produced by other individual speakers, each of whom is unique.[10]

These difficulties hinge on a more basic, and more heatedly debated, linguistic argument. Actually, the argument is a cognitive one; it attempts to determine how we think. Jerry Fodor has propounded that humans cannot learn a language (English, French, Russian) unless they know a language; that is, that there is an underlying language of thought based on representation that allows the learning of a natural language. He uses as an analogy a computer. A computer has an input/output language that allows communication between itself and its environment, but it also has a machine language—an internal, unseen, (by most users) language that allows it to use its input/output language. A human, then, has an innate language that allows the translation of representation into some natural language for communication with other humans.[11] Michael Devitt and Kim Sterelny, on the other hand, assert that learning a public (natural) language gives a person a language to think in. They state most human thought manifests itself as mental sentences in a public language. The very concept of a sentence, they add, is problematic because it is a name given to a complex process for which simplified explanatory rules have been formulated.[12]

Other linguists and psychologists have entered this fray. One point upon which most agree, including Fodor and Devitt and Sterelny, is that thought is representational. Where they differ is related to the composition, the makeup, of the representation. Is it in the form of a natural language or some other innate language? The argument may never be resolved; what is important here is that not every human being will share the precise representational perception with every other human being. Therefore, what is formulated as a natural language sentence, say in English, may vary from person to person. Because of the possibility of variance there can be misunderstanding. This can occur even when the representations are, at the core, identical and the translations into the natural language differ. In a language such as English this is less likely to happen with objects, which have accepted definitional meanings. It is more possible with ideas, for which representations may be less clear, less concrete. It is possible, for instance, for a reader to interpret a section of this book in a way I had not intended. The reason is likely to be that our representations of the idea differ. When this occurs at a nontrivial level—when the differences in linguistic expressions of a representation inhibit the inference of meaning—the result is noise. In fact, noise generated by one sentence or passage may create further noise that affects acceptance of the totality of the message. Subtle though this may be, it is a hazard to communication. Colin Cherry articulates this problem:

The writer or speaker does not communicate his *thoughts* to us; he communicates a representation for carrying out this function, under the severe discipline of using the only materials he has, sound and gesture. Speech is like painting, a representation made out of given materials—sound or paint. The function of speech is to stimulate and set up thoughts in us having correspondence with the speaker's desires; he has then communicated with us. But he has not transmitted a copy of his thoughts, a photograph, but only a stream of speech—a substitute made from the unpromising material of sound.[13]

INTERNAL NOISE

We are constantly making assumptions about ourselves and others. One of the common assumptions is that human beings are rational creatures and, as such, will normally behave rationally. For the most part, behavior is rational and is based on a set of shared beliefs and on common agreement on certain "facts." What, then, happens when we are faced with irrational or, what is more often the case, nonrational behavior? If such behavior occurs in others we may attempt to seek an explanation based on rationality. This is doomed to failure because of the essential opposition of rationality and nonrationality. However, we do resort to rational explanations because we have certain rules or modes of behavior that are designed by rational thought. This is not accidental, nor is it mere convenience; it is the basic means by which sentient beings absorb and assimilate information and relate to their environment. This is a basic tenet of any open system and is at the heart of Robert Van Gulick's observations regarding rationality:

The rationality of the system must be reflected not only in the overall consistency and coherence of its set of contents *at a time*, but also in the procedures which govern the transitions in the system's set of states *over time*. . . . The constraints of rationality . . . are elements essential to viewing any system as realizing sentential states. As such they are a special case of the general requirement noted earlier for an information possessing system to mirror or preserve the relational structure of the information which it possesses.[14]

If we accept that rationality is a deductive phenomenon, formulating propositions on the premises of what we already know, then nonrational behavior presents a dilemma. It is not based on these premises; therefore, the formulation of applicable propositions is less probable. While rationality is not absolute consistency, it tries to minimize inconsistency. Yet inconsistency is exactly what nonrational behavior presents. In order to gain an understanding of nonrational behavior, the individual would have to discover the premises, likely to be nonlogical, on which the behavior is based. While these premises are not infinite, they depart sufficiently from logical premises as to make their discovery virtually impossible by rational means. Attempting to force a rational explanation on such behavior would lead to the impasse described by Daniel C. Dennett: "Inconsistency, when discovered, is of course to be eliminated one way or another, but making the rooting out of inconsistency the pre-eminent goal of a cognizer would lead to swamping the cognitive system in bookkeeping and search operations to the exclusion of all other modes of activity."[15]

What are the individual's options, then? One is to forgo rationality and to seek a nonrational explanation. As has already been stated, the probability of the success of such an attempt would be minimal. The alternative is to treat such behavior as noise—something interfering with a message which, if unavoidable, is ignored. The result is that the message is lost. When one person says to another, "I can't talk to you when you're not rational," the admission is that noise is overwhelming and that no message is being received. Nonrational behavior in communication can be a result of confusion or a lack of understanding. For any person to make use of that rational system known as the library, the person's approach must be rational. This dilemma works two ways. For a rational user to make sense of the library there must first be an understanding of the rationality of the system. The lack of understanding also functions as internal noise. In later discussion of noise and the library/librarian we will delve into this more deeply.

PSYCHOLOGICAL NOISE

Certain kinds of information have pronounced effects on human behavior. Bad news and good news lead to mood swings that may, at times, be extreme. Of interest here, however, is not the content of information, but the amount. In actuality it is difficult to cut so fine a line between content and volume. As Jesse Shera says, "Communication becomes mere idle chatter if there is not something worth transmitting."[16] Recall that at the center of Shera's diagram of culture is communication (Figure 6.1), the transmission of thought is of essential importance at all cultural levels. Shera is wise enough in his writing to recognize that the effects of the increasing volume of communication are neither uniform nor contributory in the growth of knowledge.

> We talk glibly of the "knowledge explosion," but it is not an explosion at all. An explosion is spherical, it exerts pressure in all directions; but the growth of our accumulated knowledge is not spherical, it is amorphous. Some areas of knowledge grow much faster and extend much farther into the unknown than do others; some may be said to grow scarcely at all. Moreover, our knowledge has not expanded as rapidly as we might like to think, but we are threatened by a paper flood.
>
> One could argue that it is our *ignorance*, or at least our awareness of our ignorance, that is "exploding," rather than our knowledge.[17]

Such a realization is not universal. It cannot be or there would be no problem to complain of. In fact, the response to overload by society is to produce more. The implicit hope is that good information will drive out the bad, but it is bad information, more often than not, that obscures the good. Theodore Roszak notes, "We labor under the misconception that it is better to have too much information than too little."[18] We seem to believe that the more we have, the more selective we will be able to be. We do not understand that, if information theory is correct and information and entropy are identical measures, we are creating an ever more disordered state. The process of selection cannot keep pace with the process of production. To use Richard Saul Wurman's metaphor, "We are like a thirsty person who has been condemned to use a thimble to drink from a fire hydrant."[19] If these statements are true, then we are fated to share the combined punishments of the mythological characters of Tantalus and Sisyphus, who could see the things they desired, but could not grasp them.

Chapter 2 noted the output of information and the level of library acquisitions. Discussion in this chapter will not reiterate those specific examples; it will, instead, focus on the possible effects of the libraries' information on the users and use of libraries, primarily that of noise due to overload. There are some assumptions that underlie any concept of overload, including information overload. The most basic—and the most obvious—is that for overload to be possible, the system must have a finite capacity. In a library this is defined by factors such as money, physical space, and demand. Libraries with small budgets feel this limitation keenly. Even the rhetoric emanating from large libraries bemoans the constraints placed on their ability to grow by the budget authority. More is produced than can be acquired. The questions asked include: If we can't buy everything, what should we buy? If we can't own it, can we have access to it? Can resource sharing bail us out of this mess?

While libraries complain about the dilemma they face, they have a far greater capacity than do individual users. George Miller reviews a substantial body of research on information processing and concludes that "the span of absolute judgment and the span of immediate memory impose severe limitations on the amount of information that we are able to receive, process, and remember."[20] This is due, in part, to physiological factors. As Richard Meier states,

> In any natural environment, the eye is continually bombarded with more stimuli than the brain can process; and the more complex the environment, the more interesting it becomes—unless it contains evidence of

threat. . . . The communications system inside the organism—the brain and its sensory contacts—can be pressed to the point of confusion.[21]

This physiological limitation leads to psychological responses. An individual, when faced with overload, must choose some means of dealing with the problem. The alternative chosen depends upon the manifestation of the overload. A person at home with a window open may shut that window if street noise creates interference. Further, that person may turn up the volume on the television or stereo so that a desired stimulus replaces the undesired ones. The alternative is living with the noise, which heightens a sense of frustration and tension.

Overload can be much more complex than that, though. As Orrin Klapp says, "Noise need not be random and senseless; perfectly good information, even an organized message, can act like noise when it interferes with or disturbs reception of some signal."[22] Klapp could easily have been describing a library. The result, as Klapp sees it, is meaning lag, which has been diagrammed earlier. The metaphor he uses is that of a fast horse (the production of information) and a slow horse (consumption of information). A response to the disparity between the two has been, paradoxically, to speed up the fast horse—that is, to find better and faster ways of storing and retrieving information. Advances in microcomputers and workstations are smiled upon because the fast horse gets even faster. Conversely, though, the slow horse has been able to speed up at a much smaller increment. The result is the puzzling predicament of consumers applauding the widening gap between production and consumption. One reason for this may be a factor of overload itself: the consumer can see that consumption is increasing; but, by focusing on that, cannot perceive the widening gap. In information theory terms, the consumer is aware of the increase in choice, but is unaware that it equates to an increase in entropy.

In 1802 William Wordsworth wrote the following:

For a multitude of causes unknown to former times are now acting with a combined force to blunt the discriminating powers of the mind, and, unfitting it for all voluntary exertion, to reduce it to a state of almost savage torpor. The most effective of these causes are the great national events which are daily taking place, and the increasing accumulation of men in cities, where the uniformity of their occupations produces a craving for extraordinary incident which the rapid communication of intelligence hourly gratifies.[23]

These words show that, nearly two centuries ago (and before large-scale mechanization of printing), people were afflicted with information overload and, furthermore, were apparently not dealing with it well. An effect that has been noticed is the magnitude of demands on attention. In a 1902 letter to William Dean Howells, Henry James wrote (italics are James's):

The *faculty of attention* has utterly vanished from the general anglo-saxon mind, extinguished at its source by the big blatant Bayadère of Journalism, of the newspaper and the *picture* (above all) magazine; who keeps screaming, "Look at *me*, I am the thing, and I only, the thing that will keep you in relation with me *all the time*, without your having to attend *one minute* of the time.". . . Illustration, loud simplifications and *grossissements*, . . . the prose that is careful to be in the tone of, and with the distinction of a newspaper or bill-poster advertisement—these, and these only, meseems, "stand a chance."[24]

James was particularly concerned with the prominence of the image over the word—something not unheard of today in the context of reading and television. Clifton Fadiman brought these observation together in 1949 and assessed that "the faculty of attention in general is undergoing a wholesale displacement away from ideas and abstractions toward things and techniques."[25] Fadiman's judgment fits well with the fast horse metaphor and with much of library operations today. Much time, energy, and concentration in libraries go to storage and retrieval, specifically to making more available faster. I do not mean for a moment to denigrate this effort; in the contrary, it is an essential endeavor for libraries and librarians. It should be accompanied, though, by thought given to *what* is being stored and retrieved.

Overload exists: that is undeniable. The noise resulting from it demands some response from the individual, some manifestation of which may be conscious, some not. Some of the responses are psychological and may be analogous to defense mechanisms adopted when faced with problems or threats. James Miller outlines some of these means of adjustment that organisms employ to retain or regain coherence (or at least to avoid incoherence):

> (a) omission—temporary nonprocessing of information; (b) error—processing incorrect information, which may enable the system to return to normal processing afterwards; (c) queuing—delaying the response during a period of high overlap of input information in the expectation that it may be possible to catch up during a lull; (d) filtering—neglecting to process certain categories of information while processing others; (e) cutting categories of discrimination—responding in a general way to the input, but with less precision than would be done at lower rates, i.e., instead of reporting "I see yellow," saying "I see a light color" or "I see a color"; (f) employing multiple channels—processing information through two or more parallel channels at the same time; decentralization is a special case of this; and (g) escape from the task.[26]

Noise created by overload is a social phenomenon; it affects systems and organisms. For instance, networks, organizations, and independent producers are responsible for a preponderance of cable stations available to the average viewer. The sheer bulk of offerings can easily lead to overload, which is a source of noise to the potential viewer. One particular response may be to forego cable service entirely. On a larger scale, responses to the situation could have an effect on social communication. Because of the social nature of the problem, certain factors, activities, and enterprises may be especially affected by noise. Klapp has formulated a number of hypotheses regarding the relationship of noise and social entities, some of which are presented here:

6. The larger and more complex the system, the less chance there is for overload by social noise of the system *as a whole* because of diversity of channels, adjustment processes, and deciders.

8. Social noise is high where markets are highly developed, bringing diversified products and competitive pressures to buy and make economic decisions.
9. Social noise is high where technological innovation is rapid, forcing adjustment and new skills (whether work or leisure) on people.
10. The more highly developed a media system and the greater its output, the more chance of overload by social noise.
26. Those with access to and responsibility for large stores of information are more prone to noise overload. (Examples: researchers, librarians, book sales clerks, book buyers, news reporters, advanced students)
27. Professions processing information rapidly are more subject to noise overload. For example, doctors process information faster than do farmers; scientists are more likely to suffer overload than are technologists, who get most of their knowledge from textbooks.
29. Professions requiring much public exposure or contact with large clienteles experience more noise overload than do professions with minimal public contact and small clienteles.
31. Agencies and persons handling urgent problems are subject to social noise overload.[27]

Now that we have some background on the phenomenon of noise, we can investigate how it insinuates itself into the lives of libraries, librarians, and users.

NOISE AND THE LIBRARY

As is mentioned above, the library itself is a victim of noise. Published output alone exceeds the acquisition capabilities of virtually every library. Add to that the growth of information in other media, particularly electronic (such as video) and machine-readable formats, and libraries face the same dilemma as individuals. What to acquire; how to spend the available money? To further complicate matters, libraries are subject to some of the social complications Klapp speaks of: libraries frequently serve large and heterogeneous clienteles; their products and services are becoming more diversified; technological change is a reality; and many users have urgent needs. The difficulties faced by libraries in terms of what is rapidly becoming entropic production of information (more and more choices available) are exacerbated by an effectively shrinking pool of resources. If the curves of information production and library resources were plotted, they would look very much like Klapp's production and consumption curves. The library's ability to consume is based largely on economics; it cannot acquire simply because materials are being produced. Consumption, then, is somewhat independent of production. The gap between the two, as Klapp indicates, is widening. Is this gap also a representation of meaning lag? It is likely, in fact, to be just that. Only a portion of the output can be collected by a given library and, for the vast majority of libraries in the United States, that portion is very small. To use Klapp's metaphor, the library is the slow horse, unable to keep pace with the fast horse of production.

Still, libraries offer users more than they can get from other sources. Few individuals can afford to pay for as much information as a library can, so people gravitate to libraries for what libraries can offer them. In writing about social communication and the city, Karl Deutsch states,

> People come to large cities because there, among other reasons, they find a wider range of choice within their individual limitations than they are likely to find anywhere else. Inevitably this means that every metropolis must offer each of its residents enough freedom for a wide range of choices to be significant to them; and this also means enough freedom so that serious problems of peak loads and of recurrent, possibly growing, overloads are imposed on the city's many but limited facilities.[28]

There is an analogy here to the library—it provides choice to people, but the more effectively it does its job, the more pressure is put on it as a system. The library's input, throughput, and output can become unbalanced and, in such a state of disequilibrium, something must give. This is a foreign notion to libraries, which have attempted to be more to more people by offering more services and a greater variety of media. The result is overload to both the library and its public. In short, a library that succeeds at what it does can become a victim of its own success.

When many demands are placed on the library the demands can become overload, which results in noise. Unfortunately, there seems to be a lack of awareness of the concepts of channel capacity and overload when applied to libraries. This is reflected in official American Library Association policy. Section 1.3 of ALA's "Organization and Operational Policies" states:

> ALA will promote efforts to ensure that every individual has access to needed information at the time needed and in a format the individual can utilize, through provision of library and information services.
>
> Goals:
>
> 1. All individuals have equal access to libraries and information services.
> 2. Instruction in information use is available to all.
> 3. Government information is widely and easily available.
> 4. Library collections are developed, managed, and preserved to provide access to users to the full range of available knowledge and information.
> 5. Access to information is facilitated by bibliographic organization.
> 6. Library use is high.
> 7. Fees are not a barrier to library access and service.[29]

There is no doubt that these are admirable goals, but are they attainable, and at what cost? Cost here is not limited to financial outlay (although that is an important consideration). What are the organizational costs associated with trying to reach such goals? What are the social costs (remember that almost all libraries are segments of larger parent organizations that are faced with demands from many other segments)? What is the cost to the user, directly or indirectly, for the availability of information and services? These questions are neither rhetorical nor trivial, and are integral to the functioning of the library as a communication system.

As a communication system the library exists for the user, who must also deal with overload and noise. Does the library diminish or create noise for the user? No blanket statement is adequate to answer this question. Generally, libraries attempt to decrease noise (whether the effort is deliberately focused or not) through cataloging and classification. These functions are designed to impose a structure on the wealth of information housed in a library by describing the physical items, providing intellectual connections among various vessels of content, and by grouping like items together. All of this has a logical basis in that a user should be able to deduce that two books that share a subject heading or share elements of a call number are related in content. In many instances this works very well; the user can browse subject headings or shelves to find similar information in different packages.

In other instances, though, there are problems. Is it useful, for example, for users to consult the subject heading "Education"? This is tantamount to asking for overload. The output of such a search would be overwhelming and would prevent almost entirely the retrieval of usable information. Imagine going to an art museum and coming upon a collage, twenty feet wide and ten feet high, with hundreds of separate and only marginally related images on it. How easy is it to focus on one image? The rest of the images create noise that makes isolation very difficult. To focus on one, a person must consciously block out the others—a process that may interfere with concentration on the one image. The same can be true of such massive information retrieval. With so many choices, discrimination is an arduous task. Retrieval is further complicated by the fact that, on average, a book is assigned only a couple of subject headings. Is this adequate for a 600-page interdisciplinary collection of essays? In the past this has been a storage problem. The card catalog had to be constrained because libraries have finite and limited space to house it. In earlier days of automation storage was much more expensive and bulky than it is now. Still, even though storage is not the technical problem it once was, enhanced access would likely be expensive for a library to provide because of the increased intellectual effort it would require to provide more exhaustive access to each item. The horns of a dilemma.

What this amounts to is something of a tradeoff of costs. The library cannot afford to provide such access, so the cost is transferred to the user. One manifestation of this cost is noise. The user must deal with the limitations of access, the constraints of the subject headings (i.e., the language of Library of Congress, Sears, etc., which may not reflect the user's language), and the plethora of access points (the catalog for books, the many bibliographic indexes, and databases of other information). This may sound like an overly harsh assessment of the library. It is true that, with limited and usually inadequate resources, the library is in a genuine bind between providing as much information as possible and providing meaningful access to the information. Some libraries are applying creative problems solving to the predicament. A few libraries have added commercially available files of information and even locally created databases to their online catalogs so that users can search for various media and sources more efficiently. Some of these libraries are experimenting with natural language retrieval as well. These steps are designed to minify noise and enhance the communication process.

This is becoming an ever more crucial task for libraries. While more is being produced, more is not necessarily better from the user's standpoint. Libraries will have to cease their often uncritical pixilation with size. Public libraries, as a rule, have little conceptual difficulty with weeding; special libraries are probably even more committed to leanness when it comes to ownership of information. Academic libraries, especially larger libraries, are far too fixated on numbers for the sake of numbers. What is required is greater attention to the end product—use. This means realizing the effects of noise on retrieval as a result of overload. Browsing, for instance, does not benefit from the presence of physical items or bibliographic records of those items that no longer serve valid communication purposes. Granted, there is a need for an archival function in the library community, but this is precisely where cooperation among libraries can benefit users. There are many other aspects of this issue, such as centralization versus decentralization of collections, and there are cost considerations attached to each. The plea here is that the cost to the user and to the communication process be weighed along with everything else.

It was stated earlier that internal noise may be a function of rationality, which implies that optimum success occurs when both the user and the library are rational. This is related to the issue of cost to the user since, if the user is rational but the library is not, the cost may be high. The concept is more complex than that, though. The library, we may agree, is basically a rational structure; it functions according to a set of pre-determined rules, almost as a language does. The problem is that every language has rules; that does not mean that an English-speaking person can automatically understand German. A knowledge of the rules is required for there to be understanding. The same is true of the library. It may have sound, rational rules, but the user may not have a knowledge of those rules. The effect on the user is that he or she must then deduce or infer rules from what is presented. If there is any contradiction, the task is made much more difficult. The library then becomes a noisy channel to such a person and, so, is very difficult to interpret. There exists a link between the perceiver and the perceived; that link is necessary for understanding. Richard Palmer, in noting the centrality of this concept to hermeneutics, writes,

> Meaning is a matter of context; the explanatory procedure provides the arena for understanding. . . . Significance is a relationship to the listener's own projects and intentions. . . . To speak of an object apart from a perceiving subject is a conceptual error caused by an inadequate realistic concept of perception and the world. . . . Another way of saying this is

to state: Explanatory interpretation makes us aware that explanation is contextual, is "horizontal." It must be made within a horizon of already granted meanings and intentions.[30]

This explanatory process is becoming increasingly complex, in part because the contexts of relationships are blurred and sometimes multidimensional. This is manifest in some practical functions of libraries, not the least of which is access through subject cataloging and classification. Classification in particular is bound to be problematic since it is discrete; one physical item can be assigned only one classification, one call number. K. J. McGarry points out the difficulty inherent in this: "Like Kuhn's paradigm of scientific change classification schemes become inadequate as new knowledge and new interrelationships between subjects begin to detract from their explanatory powers."[31] What this means is that classification schedules are subject to precisely the fallacy Palmer writes of—the actuality of classification is at odds with the perception of the user. This dilemma prompts Charles T. Meadow to write, "There *has* to be a better way for users to communicate about their needs. We cannot continue to use classification and index systems that are unknown or meaningless to users."[32]

The success of user–library communication will depend on the extent that the user can understand the context. Naturally this is problematic from both perspectives: the user will not be aware of the complete set of rules under which the library operates and will have to learn or be instructed in those rules relevant to a particular type of use; the library must be aware of the other functional rules likely to be familiar to the user and express its own rules in a context understandable to the user. One way for the latter to occur may be for the library to employ technology to take better advantage of a natural language approach to its catalog. This is not offered blithely; a great deal of development is necessary before this can become a reality. Rather, it is suggested as a possible direction for future library automation consideration. One reality is that, if more extensive and broader based use is to be made of the library, the library itself needs to take the lead in fostering its own utility.

NOISE AND THE LIBRARIAN

Much that was just said about the library applies also to the librarian. In fact, it is difficult to separate the two; the reader should recognize that the distinctions made by having two sections of this chapter are somewhat artificial. That caveat offered, there is some legitimacy in looking at the institution and the people who are part of the institution. A fruitful starting point may be to come to some understanding of the users of information, especially those who are faced with more information than is easily assimilated. A good example of this is what Robert K. Merton calls the "Matthew effect," which, he says, "may serve to heighten the visibility of contributions to science by scientists of acknowledged standing and to reduce the visibility of contributions by authors who are less well known."[33] He takes the appellation from a passage of the Gospel According to St. Matthew: "For unto every one that hath shall be given, and he shall have abundance; but from him that hath not shall be taken away even that which he hath" (Matt. 25:29). "Put in less stately language, the Matthew effect consists in the accruing of greater increments of recognition for particular scientific contributions to scientists of considerable repute and the withholding of such recognition from scientists who have not yet made their mark."[34] This is a response of individuals who live in a noisy world. The response to this kind of noise is to remember what is already known—the name of the productive and recognized scientist—and to not retain what is not previously known.

Given that people exhibit certain responses to noise, the role of the librarian is accentuated. A library's catalog, even a state-of-the-art online catalog, can do only so much to interact with the user. That individual will still have some questions—about function or about content—that cannot be answered by such limited interaction. For instance, the catalog offers no evaluative assessment about an information source. The librarian's role as gatekeeper, discussed in a previous chapter, becomes an important communication mechanism. The question asked with regard to the library can be restated here: Does the librarian diminish or create noise? The reference function is designed to decrease noise; it is a process of evaluation and selection, of determining the most appropriate means of reponding to a query. To an extent, this is the function of collection development as well—selecting and acquiring information based on a knowledge of the community and its needs and desires. This is the ideal; the actual may depart from this model. Of course part of the departure from the ideal is due to the bulk of available information. Just as it is difficult for the user to assimilate the enormous body of information, so, too, is it difficult for the librarian to evaluate an ever-growing amount produced. In order to be most efficient, a library would need a platoon of subject specialists, so that the information might be subdivided into manageable proportions.

This is not a realistic possibility, so librarians are, more frequently, experts on the structure of a database (whatever its medium), not its content. In this profession we use terms like "precision" and "recall" with regard to information retrieval and feel that in the best of all worlds we maximize both. This appears to be the thinking of Marcia Bates, who argues against establishing an arbitrary target for a perfect online search, stating that in the interest of limitation much may be lost.[35] There is some truth in this; there is no perfect number that describes the apotheosis of the online search, but, as Mary Biggs points out,

> As [Bates] says, an arbitrary length limit may result in a deficient search, but she misses the poignancy of that fact for the information seeker saddled with a human "channel capacity" so much punier than a computer's. Further, she allows her notion of perfection to be delimited by current system capabilities and never suggests, when itemizing the means of shortening search output (combine terms with Boolean operators, limit by date, etc.), that more, and more responsive, means are sorely needed.[36]

The heart of the question centers around the notion of providing all relevant information to users. If librarians can accept the gatekeeper role in the realm of collection development, why can they not do the same in direct transactions with users? Why is noise reduced in one instance and increased in the other?

Part of the answer to these questions is more of an excuse than a reason. Budgets are tight, there is usually not sufficient personnel to handle all that the library would like to do, and there is a tendency to think that technology can do some of what people cannot. The last assumes much more intelligence in existing systems than is actually resident in them. As Biggs further states,

> In public services, trade-offs are forced—computers don't yet answer reference questions by themselves or educate users on their own (although they have as yet underexplored potential for doing both)—and librarians are reluctant to give up or significantly reduce any service they have traditionally provided. In many libraries, reordering priorities seems impossible.[37]

Librarians traditionally bite off more than they can chew. In the short term some things may get done, but this actually amounts to front-end overload. By attempting to provide more services than they can handle, librarians lessen the utility to the user of each of the services. No one service can command the full attention of the librarian because of the overload. The librarian then becomes a noisy channel; there is too much that is attempted to be transmitted over a channel of finite capacity. If a path of less resistance is chosen—as it sometimes must be for the preservation of the entire system—this translates to noise for the user. In conducting an online search, for example, it is easier to retrieve exhaustive than selective output. If more users are served, but the service is of little value to them, then the fundamental structure of service should be reexamined.

This focuses on dysfunction, which may leave an impression that the cosmos is in disorder and all should abandon hope. Not so. The focus is so directed in order that attention can be paid to the remedy for some communication problems experienced by libraries and librarians. With the bulk of existing information, the plethora of media, and the importance placed, at least in this country, on information itself as we approach the millennium, it is difficult not to adopt a macrocommunication posture. The point of this chapter is that noise, too, is a macrophenomenon, but with microcommunication effects. Overload is a 1990s verity, and it is quite broadbased. Libraries and librarians need to understand that they are victims of overload, just as is every individual and every institution. They do not, however, have to amplify the resulting noise; they can act as modulators; they can regulate the transmission to the user. Which is the more important function, the acquisition and storage of information or the communication of specific information in the context of the specific needs of users? This is a trick question. The library must provide access to information to be effective, but its effectiveness also depends on how well the access addresses individual needs. In conversation we do not perform a brain dump and swamp the other individual with information that is neither needed nor wanted. We must take care not to perform a library dump on users.

NOTES

1. Jesse H. Shera, *Introduction to Library Science: Basic Elements of Library Service* (Littleton, CO: Libraries Unlimited, 1976), 44.
2. Ibid., 46.
3. Ibid., 50.
4. Noam Chomsky, *Rules and Representations* (New York: Columbia University Press, 1980), 230.
5. Fred I. Dretske, *Knowledge and the Flow of Information* (Cambridge: Massachusetts Institute of Technology Press, 1981), 21.
6. Orrin E. Klapp, *Overload and Boredom: Essays on the Quality of Life in the Information Society* (Westport, CT: Greenwood Press, 1986), 84.
7. Ibid., 85.
8. Paul Watzlawick, *How Real Is Real? Communication, Disinformation, Confusion* (London: Souvenir Press, 1983), 45–54.
9. Klapp, *Overload and Boredom*, 1–2.
10. R. A. Hudson, *Sociolinguistics* (Cambridge, England: Cambridge University Press, 1980), 12.

11. Jerry A. Fodor, *The Language of Thought* (Cambridge, MA: Harvard University Press, 1975).

12. Michael Devitt and Kim Sterelny, *Language and Reality: An Introduction to the Philosophy of Language* (Cambridge, Massachusetts Institute of Technology Press, 1987), 115–29.

13. Colin Cherry, *On Human Communication: A Review, a Survey, and a Criticism*, 3rd ed. (Cambridge: Massachusetts Institute of Technology Press, 1978), 74.

14. Robert Van Gulick, "Functionalism, Information and Content," in *Mind and Cognition: A Reader*, ed. William G. Lycan (Cambridge, MA: Basil Blackwell, 1990), 117.

15. Daniel C. Dennett, "Making Sense of Ourselves," in *Mind and Cognition: A Reader*, ed. William G. Lycan (Cambridge, MA: Basil Blackwell, 1990), 193.

16. Jesse Shera, *Introduction to Library Science: Basic Elements of Library Service* (Littleton, CO: Libraries Unlimited, 1976), 197.

17. Ibid., 58–59.

18. Theodore Roszak, *The Cult of Information* (New York: Pantheon, 1986), 115.

19. Richard Saul Wurman, *Information Anxiety* (New York: Doubleday, 1989), 36.

20. George A. Miller, "The Magical Number Seven, Plus or Minus Two: Some Limits on our Capacity for Processing Information," *Psychological Review*, 63 (March 1956), 95.

21. Richard L. Meier, "Communication Stress," *Annual Review of Ecology and Systematics*, 3 (1972), 311.

22. Orrin E. Klapp, "Meaning Lag in the Information Society," *Journal of Communication*, 32 (Spring 1982), 62.

23. Quoted in Clifton Fadiman, "The Decline of Attention," *Saturday Review of Literature*, 32 (6 August 1949), 20.

24. Ibid.

25. Ibid.

26. James G. Miller, "Information Input Overload and Psychopathology," *American Journal of Psychiatry*, 116 (February 1960), 697.

27. Orrin E. Klapp, *Opening and Closing: Strategies of Information Adaptation in Society* (Cambridge: Cambridge University Press, 1978), 75–79.

28. Karl W. Deutsch, "On Social Communication and the Metropolis," *Daedalus*, 90 (Winter 1961), 101–02.

29. *ALA Handbook of Organization* (Chicago: American Library Association, 1990), 235.

30. Richard E. Palmer, *Hermeneutics* (Evanston: Northwestern University Press, 1969), 24.

31. K. J. McGarry, *Knowledge and the Librarian* (Hamden, CT: Linnet Books and Clive Bingley, 1975), 16.

32. Charles T. Meadow, "Forum: Communication in Library and Information Science," *Canadian Journal of Information Science*, 12 (1987), 7.

33. Robert K. Merton, "The Matthew Effect in Science," *Science*, 159 (January 5, 1968), 62.

34. Ibid., 58.

35. Marcia J. Bates, "The Fallacy of the Perfect Thirty-Item Online Search," *RQ*, 24 (Fall 1984), 43–50.

36. Mary Biggs, "Information Overload and Information Seekers: What We Know about Them, What to Do about Them," *The Reference Librarian*, nos. 25/26 (1989), 418–19.

37. Ibid., 421.

7

Conclusion

The intent of this book has been to show that we cannot isolate concepts, operations, and purposes related to libraries and librarians; the interrelationships and connections are too important to ignore and too essential not to examine them in juxtaposition. For this reason the discussions of information and communication have sought, if not a unity, then a kind of anastomosis—a realization that they are two branches of the same stem. If the stem can be identified, it may best be described as epistemology (as entity rather than as method). An extension of this relational definition suggests that other branches would include cognition, linguistics, hermeneutics (in the sense of explanation and interpretation), and, by further extension, culture. The analysis of information and communication as they are relevant to libraries and their users is purposely rudimentary. It is designed to spark questions and to generate the beginnings of a vision for this particular kind of communication that is sufficiently broad to spur an awareness of uses and purposes. This entails moving beyond function and operation.

Not all writers agree with this breadth of definition. John Newman, for example, states,

1. The reason that no generally accepted definition exists is not because of a lack of knowledge of communication, whether as a process, a body of knowledge, or a field of study, but because of a lack of understanding of the nature, the scope, and the function of a definition.
2. The epistemological notion that a definition must account completely for that which it defines is impractical and should be rejected.
3. Communication is so diverse and discursive that the attempt to create a generally accepted definition becomes so profoundly involved that it hinders rather than helps further thought on the subject.[1]

There is some incompleteness in Newman's stance, and some error. What is described as epistemological is actually positivist. Richard Miller describes positivism thusly:

In the broad sense, positivism is the assumption that the most important methodological notions—for example, explanation, confirmation and the identification of one kind of entity with another—can each be applied according to rules that are the same for all sciences and historical periods, that are valid a priori, and that only require knowledge of the internal content of the propositions involved for their effective application. Positivism, in this sense, is an expression of the worship of generality that has dominated philosophy at least since Kant: the idea that absolutely general, a priori rules determine what is reasonable.[2]

There is little doubt that a positivist definition of communication (or information, or many other phenomena, for that matter) would be fruitless. Just because communication is diverse does not preclude an epistemological approach to its study. Newman states explicitly that his effort at formulating a definition is pragmatic and descriptive, as though this is somehow simpler. Throughout this book only some manifestations of communication in libraries have been described. A descriptive definition is doomed to failure *because* of the multifarious nature of communication. As Alvin Goldman notes, "Epistemology is normative, evaluative, and critical, not descriptive," and, "*Empirical* sciences are not needed."[3] This approach, then, holds the promise for the study of communication in libraries and this book is a first step in that direction.

Quite a bit of attention has been paid in these pages to language—its inherent structure, its relationship to thought, its problems, and its opportunities. Though it is constantly used, language and its operations are not well understood by its speakers. Linguists such as Chomsky maintain that one reason for this is its innate nature and the ability of humans to employ a structure that is imperfectly apprehended. Such a view of language is not new. Ludwig Wittgenstein wrote,

> Man possesses the ability to construct languages capable of expressing every sense, without having any idea how each word has meaning or what its meaning is—just as people speak without knowing how the individual sounds are produced.
>
> Everyday language is a part of the human organism and is no less complicated than it.
>
> It is not humanly possible to gather immediately from it what the logic of language is.
>
> Language disguises thought. So much so, that from the outward form of the clothing it is impossible to infer the form of the thought beneath it, because the outward form of the clothing is not designed to reveal the form of the body, but for entirely different purposes.
>
> The tacit conventions on which the understanding of everyday language depends are enormously complicated.[4]

Parts of Wittgenstein's thesis are contrary to the position of Fodor and some others, but the relationship between language and thought is a particularly difficult one to discern and the debate regarding the existence and constitution of a language of thought will probably rage for many years to come. What is important about Wittgenstein's assessment is the complexity of language and its study. This is no less true of language and libraries.

In fact, libraries, as we have seen, present some particular difficulties because of some necessary structure. Natural language processing has a great deal of flexibility, and the potential for richness of expression, but it also contains a substantial potential for ambiguity (remember that English, for example, is only 50 percent redundant). As Frank Land writes, "Formal languages, such as mathematical notation, or programming languages can be very precise, but may lack facilities for coping with a wide range of concepts. A concept such as 'good' cannot be expressed by a programming language."[5] A library's classification scheme and much of its cataloging practices constitute a similar kind of formal language. Classification exists to communicate a specific and unique physical location for each item. Moreover, most classification schemes are designed to group like items together. Within these parameters classification is successful. It is also limited, however, since one item can have only one classification. Such a limitation especially hinders browsing of inter- or multidisciplinary items. Enter subject cataloging, whose purpose is to expand intellectual access to physical vessels of information. To an extent the subject access is successful, but is limited by the language of subject headings (which aim at specificity, but contain some ambiguity) and by the number of subject headings assigned to any given item. As has been stated, some libraries are experimenting with natural language processing. In examining natural language as an alternative, we have to be aware that current cataloging structure is not particularly amenable to extensive natural language processing and that natural language does contain inherent ambiguity. Will this ambiguity overwhelm the flexibility? This question is central to determining whether access will be helped or hindered and must be asked.

In addition to the difficulties presented by language, attention should be paid to the mechanism by which messages are transmitted and received. This problem is tiered; the producer of the information finds the appropriate means of transmission and then the library and librarian assist with the transmission and reception process. K. J. McGarry asks some important questions regarding this function:

> [The author] chooses his medium, it may be a book or a journal article, an audiotape or a visual signal which acts as a channel. Does the library act as a secondary channel? Would the audience be impeded in receiving the message if libraries did not exist? Is the library purely a passive

channel? Or does it act in a more active sense as an agency?—a concept much favored by Jesse Shera.[6]

Shera's thought, of course, features prominently in this book.

If the library is a medium, as is maintained here, what are its features? Some have been given in the previous six chapters, but key points include the library's dependence upon other media and the fact that media have changed over the years and continue to change. These changes are broad-based; they include recent alterations in the communication process that have resulted in greater emphasis on and attention to visual media and, to some extent, changes in what is communicated. The implications of this are that we have seen a metamorphosis of both source and receiver that stem from the media themselves. This is what Marshall McLuhan meant when he wrote, "The medium is the message."[7] The ascendent medium tends to transform not only the business of communication, but its very nature as well. McLuhan offers an analaogy that illustrates the transformation well:

> The railway did not introduce movement or transportation or wheel or road into human society, but it accelerated and enlarged the scale of previous human functions, creating totally new kinds of cities and new kinds of work and leisure. This happened whether the railway functioned in a tropical or a northern environment, and is quite independent of the freight or content of the railway medium. The airplane, on the other hand, by accelerating the rate of transportation, tends to dissolve the railway form of the city, politics, and association, quite independently of what the airplane is used for.[8]

The library may be an integral part of a new kind of transformation. Enough has been written on the "information age" that anything stated here would probably be superfluous. Central to the communication aspect of this new age is the technological development that allows remote access to an abundance of information. Rhetoric in libraries includes such concepts as a "library without walls," expanded reference services, and improved document delivery. If this transformation is realized on a substantial scale, the communication process will be undeniably altered. The language of libraries will have to change in order to make sense to users who are not in the presence of the physical organization of a library or of the artifacts. Here we assume that, for the short term at least, many of the traditional functions and collections of libraries will continue.

The issues associated with *access* to information, remote or otherwise, also impinge on how the library looks at information. What seems to be emerging is something of a bifurcated information base: on the one hand an array of databases of varying types that can be accessed by the library for users or, in many cases, directly by the users themselves and, on the other, a collection of physical items, many of which are in demand and are heavily used. The vision of the library for the foreseeable future must include both of these. Keep in mind that "library" is used in the broadest terms; certainly some individual libraries will gravitate to one end or the other of the spectrum, but the library in the generic sense will depend on both extensions of the base. Realization of this tempers the rhetoric of information. Some writers assert that information is a different kind of commodity; it can simultaneously be dispensed and retained. The library can communicate this information without giving it up; it is still available to the next user who requests it. This is true, but only to a point and only for certain kinds of information retrieval. Much of library business takes place in public libraries and much of that business is in the form of users checking out materials. If there is one copy of a title and someone has it checked out, then it is not immediately available to the next user who wants it. The same is true for much of academic library business. The moral is not to take too narrow a view of information or to extrapolate to all formats of information the properties of a few.

Breadth of vision is also important for librarians in communication with users. In earlier discussions of information theory it became obvious that much of the technical information that engineers and information technicians are concerned with is binary. Switches are either on or off; answers to questions are either yes or no. The pervasiveness of digital computer technology, especially personal computers, may serve to reinforce attentions to binary forms of information. It should be remembered, though, that binary is the simplest form of communication and that human communication is usually far from simple. With the requests made by most users there are many possibilities—possibilities increased by that aspect of language that is not redundant—that decrease the chances of success. The librarian frequently has to apply a kind of diagnostic process to answering users' questions. This generally involves a series of questions of increasing complexity aimed at linking the users' responses so as to increase the likelihood of success, somewhat like a game of twenty questions. There is a flaw with this line of reasoning: the game only works if one player knows the answer. Library communication does not fit this model; it is frequently too nebulous and elusive to expect any mechanistic approach to be effective. One reason is that user–library/librarian communication is bound by few rules. The users' requests, for example, might not be satisfied by the holdings of a given library; the requests are not limited to information that has been packaged and then acquired by the library.

Another measure of avoidance here should be the avoidance of too narrow a view of information processing. The brain is always processing information, but this activity is not a perfect parallel with thinking. As Theodore Roszak says throughout *The Cult of Information*, the mind thinks with ideas, not with information.[9] The mind does use information in the course of thinking, but more as a tool used to draw inferences. Information here is used in a sense more closely related to data—there are innumerable bits of data available; the mind selects which to retain and uses them to formulate, develop, or support ideas. This implies the existence of some kind of dualism, some distinction between brain and mind. Heinz Pagels explains this epistemic dualism in terms of the ways we reason, the ways we think about the world and our place in it.

> Kant recognized that we employ at least two different kinds of reason in coming to grips with reality, the "theoretical reason" of the scientist and

the "practical reason" of the lawyer, businessman, or just about anyone else. The theoretical reasoning of the scientist sees the world according to natural theories. In *principle*, according to theoretical reason, the world is one, and its explication can be reduced to the properties of primary elements of material existence. This is also the standpoint of the identity theorist—the mind and consciousness are a biological-material process explicable in terms of natural laws. The states of the mind are in *principle* reducible to the states of the brain.

In *practice*, as any scientist will be the first to admit, such a reduction is, in detail, impossible to achieve. Hence the necessity for practical reason, which sees the mind as autonomous and the person as a free moral agent, an agent that for most practical purposes is independent of the brain. This is the reasoning most people use in dealing with the problems of life. If a person misbehaves, we say that they have done wrong rather than that their brain is malfunctioning.

Theoretical reason, the way of science, sees the mind-body problem from the third-person perspective; practical reason sees this problem from a first-person perspective. Kant's epistemic dualism explicitly acknowledges that we see the mind-body problem differently depending on whether we view it in terms of what in *principle* must be true or in terms of what in *practice* we can achieve. And that, I believe, is how it is.[10]

If this sounds complex, it is. In fact, complexity is at the heart of this whole issue of library communication and communication in general. Brain processes are enormously complex, even though neural impulses may be simple. Complexity results from the huge number of potential impulses and the connections between them, and is evident in library communication. There is no way for a librarian to tell how a request entered the user's mind. While the mind thinks with ideas, we have to ask if the user approaches the library with a functional idea of its structure and contents that matches the functional ideas of the creators of that structure and those contents. If the idea of the user regarding the library diverges from that of its creators, can that idea be altered by the image presented by the information? When the user has an idea that prompts a question, is the idea changed when the user is presented with information? To what extent are libraries able to shape ideas through the processing and retrieval of information?

As a tool, information is powerful; as an influence, information is complex. Charles Meadow says,

> There *has* to be a better way for users to communicate about their needs. We cannot continue to use information access languages with our computer systems that require virtually full-time attention in order to maintain proficiency in their use. We cannot continue to produce supposedly educated people who cannot find the information they need to do their jobs. We cannot separate *providing* library reference service from *evaluation* of retrieved material which will affect a next round in the search process. We must provide *information counselors* whose subject knowledge approaches that of the user and who can consult on the value of retrieved information as well as on the mechanics of retrieval.
>
> The library must adopt the posture of being primarily a communication agency, not primarily a storehouse or reading room. Its purpose is to inform users about information stored within and without its walls. Its walls should play no role in determining the scope of a search or of the assistance its staff will provide.
>
> Its focus should be on *communication about information*, not the convenience of its staff or the maintenance of its collection. The concept of *holdings* must be subordinated to the concept of *accessibility*.[11]

This argument is similar to Ralph LaRossa's view of hierarchical message structures. LaRossa puts forth two propositions. "Every communicated message contains two sorts of meaning: a report and a command,"[12] and, "The command aspect of a message is of a higher logical type than the report aspect. The command aspect is, thus, meta-information."[13] The analogy relevant to the library is a restating of Meadow's assertion: The library should provide the information, but also should provide the user with some sort of instruction regarding what to do with the information. Reality is not as simple as Meadow's admonishment and LaRossa's propositions. As is true of much of human endeavor, there is a chance for success and a chance for failure. This is not a random phenomenon, but success does depend upon an understanding of the process and an understanding that more may not necessarily be better. Communication by the library to the user is a matter of providing more; other communication elements are essential to success. The best way to close this book is with one more thought of Jesse Shera: "Librarianship is one facet of the communication process by means of which a culture maintains itself; without communication there can be no culture. But communication becomes mere idle chatter if there is not something worth transmitting."[14]

NOTES

1. John B. Newman, "A Rationale for a Definition of Communication," *Journal of Communication*, 10 (June 1960), 115.
2. Richard W. Miller, *Fact and Method* (Princeton, NJ: Princeton University Press, 1987), 3.
3. Alvin I. Goldman, *Epistemology and Cognition* (Cambridge, MA: Harvard University Press, 1986), 2.
4. Ludwig Wittgenstein, *Tractatus Logico-Philosophicus*, trans. D. F. Pears and B. F. McGuinness (London: Routledge & Kegan Paul, 1961), 35–37.
5. Frank Land, "Is an Information Theory Enough? *Computer Journal*, 28, no. 3 (1985), 212.
6. K. J. McGarry, *Communication, Knowledge and the Librarian* (Hamden, CT: Linnet Books and Clive Bingley, 1975), 21.
7. Marshall McLuhan, *Understanding Media: The Extensions of Man* (New York: Signet, 1964), 23.
8. Ibid., 24.
9. Theodore Roszak, *The Cult of Information* (New York: Pantheon, 1986).
10. Heinz R. Pagels, *The Dreams of Reason* (New York: Bantam Books, 1989), 221.
11. Charles T. Meadow, "Forum: Communication in Library and Information Science," *Canadian Journal of Information Science*, 12, no. 1 (1987), 7.
12. Ralph LaRossa, "Interpreting Hierarchical Message Structure," *Journal of Communication*, 24 (Spring 1974), 62.
13. Ibid., 63.
14. Jesse H. Shera, *Introduction to Library Science* (Littleton, CO: Libraries Unlimited, 1976), 197.

Bibliography

Allwood, Carl Martin. "Anthropology of Knowledge and Cognitive Psychology." *Communication & Cognition*, 20 no. 4 1987: 295–310.

Association of Research Libraries. *ARL Statistics*. Washington, DC: Association of Research Libraries, various years.

Astle, Deana L. "The Scholarly Journal: Whence or Whither." *Journal of Academic Librarianship* 15 (July 1989): 151–56.

Bates, Marcia J. "The Fallacy of the Perfect Thirty-Item Online Search." *RQ* 24 (Fall 1984), 43–50.

Berlo, David K. *The Process of Communication*. New York: Holt, Rinehart, and Winston, 1960.

Bernier, Charles L., and A. Neil Yerkey. *Cogent Communication: Overcoming Reading Overload*. Westport, CT: Greenwood Press, 1979.

Biggs, Mary. "Information Overload and Information Seekers: What We Know about Them, What We Do about Them." *The Reference Librarian* Nos. 25/26 (1989): 411–29.

Bittner, John. *Foundations of Communication*. Englewood Cliffs, NJ: Prentice-Hall, 1985.

Blonsky, Marshall, ed. *On Signs*. Baltimore: Johns Hopkins University Press, 1985.

Boulding, Kenneth. *The Image*. Ann Arbor: University of Michigan Press, 1956.

Bowker Annual of Library and Book Trade Information. New York: R. R. Bowker, various years.

Bryson, Lyman, ed. *The Communication of Ideas*. New York: Harper & Row, 1948.

Budd, John. "The User and the Library: A Discussion of Communication." *The Reference Librarian* 20 (1987): 205–21.

Bunge, Charles A. "Interpersonal Dimensions of the Reference Interview: A Historical Review of the Literature." *Drexel Library Quarterly* 20 (Spring 1984): 4–23.

Butler, Pierce. *An Introduction to Library Science*. Chicago: Phoenix Books, University of Chicago Press, 1961.

Campbell, David P., and Dale Level. "A Black Box Model of Communication." *Journal of Business Communication* 22 (Summer 1985): 37–47.

Campbell, Jeremy. *Grammatical Man: Information, Entropy, Language, and Life*. New York: Simon & Schuster, 1982.

Campbell, Jeremy. *The Improbable Machine*. New York: Simon and Schuster, 1989.

Carroll, John B.,. ed. *Language, Thought, and Reality: Selected Writings of Benjamin Lee Whorf*. Cambridge: Massachusetts Institute of Technology Press, 1956.

Cerroni-Long, E. L. "Culture as Communication: Defining the Parameters of Analysis." *Communication & Cognition* 18, 4 (1989): 379–92.

Cherry, Colin. *On Human Communication: A Review, a Survey, and a Criticism*, 3rd ed. Cambridge: Massachusetts Institute of Technology Press, 1978.

Chomsky, Noam. *Reflections on Language*. New York: Pantheon Books, 1975.

———. *Rules and Representations*. New York: Columbia University Press, 1980.

Chrisman, Miriam Usher. *Lay Culture, Learned Culture: Books and Social Change in Strasbourg, 1480–1599*. New Haven, CT: Yale University Press, 1982.

Cleveland, Harlan. "Information as a Resource." *Futurist*, December 1982, 16.

Cohen, Michael D., James G. March, and Johan P. Olsen. "A Garbage Can Model of Organizational Choice." *Administrative Science Quarterly* 17 (March 1972): 1–25.

Cooley, Charles. *Social Organization: A Study of the Larger Mind*. New York: Scribner's, 1924.

Coutu, Walter. "An Operational Definition of Meaning." *Quarterly Journal of Speech* 48 (February 1962): 59–64.

Cresswell, John W., ed. "Measuring Faculty Research Performance." *New Directions for Institutional Research* no. 50 (June 1986).

Csikszentmihalyi, Mihalyi, and Fausto Massimini. "On the Psychological Selection of Bio-Cultural Information." *New Ideas in Psychology* 3, no. 2 (1985): 115–38.

Curley, Arthur, and Dorothy Broderick. *Building Library Collections*, 6th ed. Metuchen, NJ: Scarecrow Press, 1985.

Dance, Frank E. X., ed. *Human Communication Theory: Original Essays.* New York: Holt, Rinehart, and Winston, 1967.

Darnell, Donald K. "Clozentropy: A Procedure for Testing English Language Proficiency of Foreign Students." *Speech Monographs* 37 (March 1970): 36–46.

Deely, John. *Introducing Semiotic: Its History and Doctrine.* Bloomington: Indiana University Press, 1982.

Deutsch, Karl W. "On Communication Models in the Social Sciences." *Public Opinion Quarterly.* (1952): 16.

———. "On Social Communication and the Metropolis." *Daedalus* 90 (Winter 1961): 99–110.

Deutsch, Karl W., and Leroy N. Reiselbach. "Recent Trends in Political Theory and Political Philosophy." *Annals of the American Academy of Political and Social Science* (July 1965): 360.

Devitt, Michael, and Kim Sterelny. *Language and Reality: An Introduction to the Philosophy of Language.* Cambridge: Massachusetts Institute of Technology Press, 1987.

Dougherty, Richard M., and Laura L. Blomquist. *Improving Access to Library Resources: The Influence of Organization of Library Collections, and of User Attitudes Toward Innovative Services.* Metuchen, NJ: Scarecrow Press, 1974.

Dretske, Fred I. *Knowledge and the Flow of Information.* Cambridge: Massachusetts Institute of Technology Press, 1981.

Eco, Umberto. *Semiotics and the Philosophy of Language.* Bloomington: Indiana University Press, 1984.

———. *A Theory of Semiotics.* Bloomington: Indiana Universtiy Press, 1976.

Eisenstein, Elizabeth L. *The Printing Press as an Agent of Change: Communications and Cultural Transformations in Early-Modern Europe,* vols. 1 and 2. Cambridge, England: Cambridge University Press, 1979.

Evans, G. Edward. *Developing Library and Information Center Collections.* Littleton, CO: Libraries Unlimited, 1987.

Fadiman, Clifton. "The Decline of Attention." *Saturday Review of Literature* 32 (August 6, 1949): 20–24.

Fairthorne, Robert A. "Morphology of 'Information Flow'." *Journal of the Association for Computing Machinery* 14 (October 1967): 710–19.

Finn, Seth, and Donald F. Roberts. "Source, Destination, and Entropy: Reassessing the Role of Information Theory in Communication Research." *Communication Research* 11 (October 1984): 453–76.

Fodor, Jerry A. *The Language of Thought.* Cambridge, MA: Harvard University Press, 1975.

Fox, Christopher John. *Information and Misinformation: An Investigation of the Notions of Information, Misinformation, Informing, and Misinforming*. Westport, CT: Greenwood Press, 1983.

Fredin, Eric S. "The Context of Communication: Interactive Telecommunication, Interpersonal Communication, and Their Effect on Ideas." *Communication Research* 10 (October 1983): 553–81.

Gerbner, George. *The Analysis of Communication Content*. New York: Wiley, 1969.

Gleick, James. *Chaos: Making a New Science*. New York: Viking, 1987.

Glogoff, Stuart. "Communication Theory's Role in the Reference Interview." *Drexel Library Quarterly* 19 (Spring 1983): 56–72.

Goldman, Alvin I. *Epistemology and Cognition*. Cambridge, MA: Harvard University Press, 1986.

Gothberg, Helen M. "Communication Patterns in Library Reference and Information Science." *RQ* 13 (Fall 1973): 7–14.

Green, Samuel S. "Personal Relations Between Librarians and Readers." *Library Journal* 1 (October 1876): 74–81.

Greimas, Algirdas Julien. *On Meaning: Selected Writings in Semiotic Theory*. Minneapolis: University of Minnesota Press, 1987.

Hamlin, Arthur T. *The University Library in the United States: Its Origins and Development*. Philadelphia: University of Pennsylvania Press, 1981.

Harary, Frank, and Mark F. Batell. "The Concept of Negative Information." *Behavioral Science* 23 (July 1978): 264–70.

Harris, Michael H. *History of Libraries in the Western World*, compact textbook edition. Metuchen, NJ: Scarecrow Press, 1984.

Harris, Michael H. "The Dialectic of Defeat: Antinomies [*sic*] in Research in Library and Information Science." *Library Trends* 34 (Spring 1986), 515–31.

Houghton, Bernard. *Scientific Periodicals: Their Development, Characteristics and Control*. Hamden, CT: Linnet Books and Clive Bingley, 1975.

Hudson, R. A. *Sociolinguistics*. Cambridge, England: Cambridge University Press, 1980.

Institute for Scientific Information. *Science Citation Index, Journal Citation Reports*. Philadelphia: ISI. various years.

Jackendoff, Ray. *Semantics and Cognition*. Cambridge: Massachusetts Institute of Technology Press, 1983.

Jackson, Sidney L. *Libraries and Librarianship in the West: A Brief History*. New York: McGraw-Hill, 1974.

Jackson, Willis, ed. *Communication Theory*. New York: Academic Press, 1953.

Just, Marcel Adam, and Patricia A. Carpenter, eds. *Cognitive Processes in Comprehension*. Hillsdale, NJ: Lawrence Erlbaum Associates, Pubs., 1977.

Kecskemeti, Paul. *Meaning, Communication, and Value.* Chicago: University of Chicago Press, 1952.

Kelly, John C. *A Philosophy of Communication.* London: Centre for the Study of Communication and Culture, 1981.

Khinchin, A. I. *Mathematical Foundations of Information Theory.* New York: Dover Publications, Inc., 1957.

Klapp, Orrin E. "Meaning Lag in the Information Society." *Journal of Communication* 32 (Spring 1982): 56–66.

———. *Opening and Closing: Strategies of Information Adaptation in Society.* Cambridge: Cambridge University Press,1978.

———. *Overload and Boredom: Essays on the Quality of Life in the Information Society.* Westport, CT: Greenwood Press, 1986.

Krippendorff, Klaus. "An Epistemological Foundation for Communication." *Journal of Communication* 34 (Summer 1984): 21–36.

Kuhn, Thomas S. *The Structure of Scientific Revolutions*, 2nd ed. Chicago: University of Chicago Press, 1970.

Land, Frank. "Is an Information Theory Enough?" *Computer Journal* 28, no. 3 (1985): 211–15.

LaRossa, Ralph. "Interpreting Hierarchical Message Structure." *Journal of Communication* 24 (Spring 1974): 61–68.

Laugher, Charles T. *Thomas Bray's Grand Design: Libraries of the Church of England in America, 1695–1785.* Chicago: American Library Association, 1973.

Littlejohn, Stephen W. *Theories of Human Communication*, 2nd ed. Belmont, CA: Wadsworth Publishing Co., 1983.

Luhmann, Niklas. "The Improbability of Communication." *International Social Science Journal* 33, no. 1 (1981): 122–32.

Lycan, William G., ed. *Mind and Cognition: A Reader.* Cambridge, MA: Basil Blackwell, 1990.

Machlup, Fritz and Una Mansfield, eds. *The Study of Information.* New York: Wiley, 1983.

MacKay, Donald M. *Information, Mechanism, and Meaning.* Cambridge: Massachusetts Institute of Technology Press, 1969.

McGarry, K. J. *Communication, Knowledge and the Librarian.* Hamden, CT: Linnet Books and Clive Bingley, 1975.

———. ed. *Mass Communication: Selected Readings for Librarians.* Hamden, CT: Linnet Books and Clive Bingley, 1972.

McLuhan, Marshall. *Understanding Media. The Extensions of Man.* New York: McGraw-Hill, 1964.

Meadow, Charles T. "Forum: Communication in Library and Information Science." *Canadian Journal of Information Science* 12, no. 1 (1987): 1–9.

Meier, Richard L. "Communication Stress." *Annual Review of Ecology and Systematics* 3 (1972), 289–314.

Merritt, Marilyn. "On Questions Following Questions in Service Encounters." *Language in Society* 5 (December 1976): 315–57.

Merton, Robert K. "The Matthew Effect in Science." *Science* 159 (January 5, 1968): 56–63.

Miller, George A. "The Magical Number Seven, Plus or Minus Two: Some Limits on Our Capacity for Processing Information." *Psychological Review* 63 (March 1956): 81–97.

———. "What Is Information Measurement?" *American Psychologist* 8 (January 1953): 3–11.

Miller, James G. "Information Input Overload and Psychopathology." *American Journal of Psychiatry* 116 (February 1960): 695–704.

Miller, Richard W. *Fact and Method: Explanation, Confirmation and Reality in the Natural and the Social Sciences*. Princeton, NJ: Princeton University Press, 1987.

Miller, Walter M. *A Canticle for Leibowitz*. New York: Bantam, 1962.

Molyneux, Robert E., comp. *ACRL University Library Statistics, 1987–1988*. Chicago: Association of College and Research Libraries, 1989.

Mooers, Calvin N. "Analysis of the Hexagon of Notification." *Journal of Documentation* 30 (June 1974): 181–94.

Murdock, John W., and David M. Liston, Jr. "A General Model of Information Transfer." *American Documentation* 18 (October 1967): 197–208.

Mutter, Sharon A., and Hashtroudi, Shahin. "Cognitive Effort and the Word Frequency Effect in Recognition and Lexical Decision." *American Journal of Psychology* 100 (Spring 1987).

Naismith, Rachael, and Joan Stein. "Library Jargon: Student Comprehension of Technical Language Used by Librarians." *College & Research Libraries* 50 (September 1989): 543–52.

Newman, John B. "A Rationale for a Definition of Communication." *Journal of Communication* 10 (June 1960): 115–24.

Ogden, C. K., and I. A. Richards. *The Meaning of Meaning: A Study of the Influence of Language Upon Thought and of the Science of Symbolism*. San Diego: Harvest/Harcourt Brace Jovanovich. 1989.

Orr, J. M. *Libraries as Communication Systems*. Westport, CT: Greenwood Press, 1977.

Osgood, Charles E. "Psycholinguistics: A Survey of Theory and Research Problems." *Journal of Abnormal and Social Psychology* 49 (October 1954).

Pagels, Heinz R. *The Dreams of Reason*. New York: Bantam Books, 1989.

Palmer, F. R. *Semantics*, 2nd ed. Cambridge: Cambridge University Press, 1981.

Palmer, Richard E. *Hermeneutics*. Evanston: Northwestern University Press, 1969.

Peirce, Charles S. *Collected Papers*. Cambridge, MA: Harvard University Press, 1969.

Percy, Walker. *The Message in the Bottle*. New York: Farrar, Straus, and Giroux, 1975.

Pierce, John R. *An Introduction to Information Science: Symbols, Signals and Noise*, rev. ed. New York: Dover Publications, Inc., 1980.

Pool, Ithiel de Sola. "Tracking the Flow of Information." *Science* 221, no. 12 (August 1983): 609–13.

Pratt, Allan D. *The Information of the Image*. Norwood, NJ: Ablex Publihsing Co., 1982.

Price, Derek J. de Solla. *Little Science, Big Science . . . and Beyond*. New York: Columbia University Press, 1986.

Rettig, James. "A Theoretical Model and Definition of the Reference Process." *RQ* 18 (Fall 1978): 19–29.

Rider, Fremont. *The Scholar and the Future of the Research Library: A Problem and Its Solution*. New York: Hadham Press, 1944.

Ritchie, David. "Shannon and Weaver: Unraveling the Paradox of Information." *Communication Research* 13 (April 1986): 278–98.

Rogers, Everett M., and D. Lawrence Kincaid. *Communication Networks: Toward a New Paradigm for Research*. New York: Free Press, 1981.

Roszak, Theodore. *The Cult of Information*. New York: Pantheon, 1986.

Ruben, Brent D., ed. *Information and Behavior*, vol. 1. New Brunswick, NJ: Transaction Books, 1985.

Rzevski, George. "On Criteria for Assessing an Information Theory." *Computer Journal* 28, no. 3 (1985): 200–2.

Saussure, Ferdinand de. *Course in General Linguistics*. New York: McGraw-Hill, 1966.

Scarrott, C. G. "Information, the Life Blood of Organisation." *Computer Journal* 28, no. 3 (1985): 203–5.

Schlachter, Gail A., ed. *The Service Imperative for Libraries: Essays in Honor of Margaret E. Monroe*. Littleton, CO: Libraries Unlimited, 1982.

Scholarly Communication: *The Report of the National Enquiry*. Baltimore: Johns Hopkins University Press, 1979.

Schramm, Wilbur, and Donald F. Roberts, eds. *The Process and Effects of Mass Communication*. Urbana: University of Illinois Press, 1971.

Sebeok, Thomas A. "Coding in the Evolution of Signalling Behavior." *Behavioral Science* 7 (October 1962): 430–32.

Sereno, Kenneth K. *Foundations of Communication Theory*. New York: Harper & Row, 1970.

Severin, Werner J., and James W. Tankard, Jr. *Communication Theories: Origins, Methods, Uses*. New York: Hastings House, 1979.

Shannon, Claude E., and Warren Weaver. *The Mathematical Theory of Communication*. Urbana: University of Illinois Press, 1949.

Shaw, W. M., Jr. "Statistical Disorder and the Analysis of a Communication-Graph." *Journal of the American Society for Information Science* 34 (March 1983): 146–49.

Shera, Jesse H. *Introduction to Library Science: Basic Elements of Library Service*. Littleton, CO: Libraries Unlimited, 1976.

Sless, David. *In Search of Semiotics*. Totowa, NJ: Barnes & Noble Books, 1986.

Smith, Mickey. "A Model of Human Communication." *IEEE Communications Magazine* 26 (February 1988): 5–14.

Smith, Ronald L. *General Models of Communication*, Special Report No. 5. West Lafayette, IN: Purdue University, Department of Speech, 1962.

Stamper, R. K. "Towards a Theory of Information: Information: Mystical Fluid or a Subject for Scientific Inquiry?" *Computer Journal* 28, no. 3 (1985): 195–99.

Stevens, Norman D. *Communication Throughout Libraries*. Metuchen, NJ: Scarecrow Press, 1983.

Stevens, S. S. "Introduction: A Definition of Communication." *Journal of the Acoustical Society of America* 22 (November 1950): 689–90.

Targowski, Andrew S., and Joel P. Bowman. "The Layer-Based, Pragmatic Model of the Communication Process." *Journal of Business Communication* 25 (Winter 1988): 5–24.

Tully, C. J. "Information, Human Activity and the Nature of Relevant Theories." *Computer Journal* 28, no. 3 (1985): 206–10.

Tutzauer, Frank. "Toward a Theory of Disintegration in Communication Networks." *Social Networks* 7 (1985): 263–85.

Vavrek, Bernard. "The Nature of Reference Librarianship." *RQ* 13 (Spring 1974): 213–17.

Waldhart, Thomas J., and Enid S. Waldhart. *Communication Research in Library and Information Science: A Bibliography on Communication in the Sciences, Social Sciences, and Technology*. Littleton, CO: Libraries Unlimited, 1975.

Watzlawick, Paul. *How Real Is Real: Communication, Disinformation, and Confusion*. London: Souvenir, 1983.

Watzlawick, Paul, Janet Helmick Beavin, and Don D. Jackson. *Pragmatics of Human Communication: A Study of Interactional Patterns, Pathologies, and Paradoxes*. New York: W. W. Norton & Co., 1967.

Weaver, Warren. "The Mathematics of Communication." *Scientific American* 181 (July 1949): 11–15.

Wiener, Norbert. *The Human Use of Human Beings: Cybernetics and Society.* New York: Houghton Mifflin, 1954.

Wilson, Patrick. *Public Knowledge, Private Ignorance: Toward a Library and Information Policy.* Westport, CT: Greenwood Press, 1977.

Wilson, Pauline. "Mission or Information: What Business Are We In?" *Journal of Academic Librarianship* 14 (May 1988): 82–86.

Winograd, Terry. "A Framework for Understanding Discourse." In *Cognitive Processes in Comprehension*, ed. Marcel Adam Just and Patricia Carpenter. Hillsdale, NJ: Lawrence Erlbaum Associates, 1977.

Winter, Michael F. *The Culture and Control of Expertise: Toward a Sociological Understanding of Librarianship.* Westport, CT: Greenwood Press, 1988.

Wittgenstein, Ludwig. *Tractatus Logico-Philosophicus.* Translated by D. F. Pears and B. F. McGuinness. London: Routledge & Kegan Paul, 1961.

Woodruff, Eleanor B. "Reference Work." *Library Journal* 22 (Conference Issue 1897): 65–67.

Wurman, Richard Saul. *Information Anxiety.* New York: Doubleday, 1989.

Zipf, George K. *Human Behavior and the Principle of Least Effort.* New York: Addison Wesley, 1949.

Index

ABOUT THE AUTHOR

JOHN M. BUDD is Associate Professor at the School of Library and Information Science at Louisiana State University. He is also the author of numerous articles that have been published in professional journals.

www.ingramcontent.com/pod-product-compliance
Lightning Source LLC
LaVergne TN
LVHW101441200926
848483LV00001B/17
* 9 7 8 0 3 1 3 2 8 1 5 3 2 *